Decolonization and Healing:
Indigenous Experiences in the United States,
New Zealand, Australia and Greenland

Prepared for

The Aboriginal Healing Foundation

by

Linda Archibald

2006

Table of Contents

TABLES

Definitions

Aboriginal people or Aboriginal - includes Métis, Inuit and First Nations, regardless of where they live in Canada and regardless of whether they are "registered" under the *Indian Act* of Canada. For this report, it also includes all other Indigenous peoples of the world.

Colonialism - control by one power over a dependent area or people.

Decolonization - to free from colonial status.

Historic trauma - is a cluster of traumatic events. Hidden collective memories of trauma, or a collective non-remembering, is passed from generation to generation, as are the maladaptive social and behavioural patterns that are symptoms of many social disorders. **Or** - is a cumulative emotional and psychological wounding across generations resulting from massive tragedies.

Legacy of physical and sexual abuse in residential schools - (often referred to as "Legacy") means the ongoing direct and indirect effects of physical and sexual abuse at residential schools. It includes the effects of Survivors, their families, descendants and communities (including communities of interest). These effects may include, and are not limited to, family violence, drug, alcohol and substance abuse, physical and sexual abuse, loss of parenting skills and self-destructive behaviour.

Post-colonial psychology - the emotional and behavioural characteristics of a colony relating to or being the time following the establishment of independence; the science (or study) dealing with the emotional, mental and behavioural characteristics of a colony relating to the establishment of independence.

Post traumatic stress disorder (PTSD) - a psychological disorder that develops in some individuals who had major traumatic experiences, such as those who experienced serious accidents, survived or witnessed violent crimes or acts of wars. Symptoms can include emotional numbness at first, depression, excessive irritability, guilt for having survived others who were injured or died, recurrent nightmares, flashback to the traumatic scene, and overreactions to sudden noises.

i

Definitions

Residential schools - The residential school system in Canada, attended by Aboriginal students. It may include industrial schools, boarding schools, homes for students, hostels, billets, residential schools, residential schools with a majority of day students, or a combination of any of the above.

Survivor - an Aboriginal person who attended and survived the residential school system in Canada.

Executive Summary

Introduction

In the 77 years between 1892 and 1969, generations of Aboriginal children in Canada were sent to government-sponsored residential schools run by the Roman Catholic, Anglican, United, Presbyterian and other churches. The physical and sexual abuse suffered by many of these children—along with the imposed alienation from families, communities and cultures—left scars that have been passed on from generation to generation. This legacy of abuse and intergenerational trauma is now well recognized. Sadly, Canada was not alone in its attempts to assimilate Aboriginal people through the education system. While educational policies and the criteria under which children were removed varied, many thousands of Indigenous children in the United States and Australia were taken away from their families and placed in boarding or mission schools. Colonialism took different forms in New Zealand and Greenland: if judged by the lower socioeconomic and health status of Indigenous people compared to non-Indigenous citizens, the consequences of colonialism were equally damaging. This report explores colonization, decolonization and healing among Indigenous people in these four nation-states.

Limitations

A full review of the literature on decolonization and healing among Indigenous people in the United States, New Zealand, Australia and Greenland is beyond the scope of this report, the analysis is based on a selection of books, journal articles, government reports and other publications available in Canada during the time this report was being developed. Considerably less information was found on Greenland because so few research studies are published in English. Also, limited information was found on Indigenous community-based healing initiatives, in part, due to the tendency of smaller projects to not publish research related to their work, no matter how innovative and successful. Knowledge within Aboriginal communities is more likely to be transmitted orally than to be included in publications available internationally.

Part I: Colonization

Part I provides a brief overview of Indigenous experiences under colonialism in the United States, New Zealand, Australia and Greenland, including a description of educational policies and their impact on

Executive Summary

Indigenous languages and cultures. This overview provides a backdrop for understanding the link between the experience of being colonized and the need for healing.

Colonization proceeded along different paths in the United States, New Zealand, Australia and Greenland. Poka Laenui (2000), an Indigenous Hawaiian, describes colonization as being a social process characterized by five distinct but interconnected phases: denial of Indigenous culture; destruction of all physical symbols of culture; denigration of Indigenous belief systems and ceremonies; tokenism, in which the remnants of culture are tolerated as folklore; and exploitation of aspects of traditional culture, such as music and art, that refuse to disappear. Various characteristics and permutations of these phases of colonization can be recognized in the history of the United States, New Zealand, Australia and Greenland—although not necessarily chronologically and not all phases are evident in every country. An overview of events related to the colonization process in each nation-state is provided.

Part II: Decolonization and Healing

Part II explores decolonization, a process that involves addressing historic trauma and unravelling the tragic aftereffects of colonization. Historic trauma theory argues that individuals can be traumatized by events that occurred before their birth. Thus, a relationship exists between history, the social, economic and political environments, and individual experiences. It follows that therapeutic approaches to healing that incorporate Indigenous history will more effectively address root causes. At the same time, many individuals need therapeutic help to heal from deeply personal wounds or to address depression, addiction or the effects of physical and sexual abuse.

A table details the juxtaposition of the sociopolitical process of decolonization, the individual process of healing from post traumatic stress disorder and healing from historic trauma. Presented in this way, the similarities between these three processes are revealed. The first column focuses on the decolonization process, a corollary of the colonization process described in Part I. The second column presents the stages of recovery from post traumatic stress disorder (PTSD). The last column—healing from historic trauma—brings history and culture together with personal healing in a journey that is both individual and collective in nature, and is based on a combination of the first two columns.

Executive Summary

This is followed by examples of the decolonization process in each of the four nation-states under discussion. In the United States, the emergence of post-colonial psychology is discussed. This provides the theoretical basis for linking PTSD and historic trauma. A description of the revival of Maori culture and traditional healing within New Zealand society follows. Remembrance and mourning are discussed with a focus on Australia. Aboriginal and Torres Strait Islander people have been struggling to come to terms with their colonial past and to have the injustice they suffered formally acknowledged by the national government. The final section looks at the success of Greenlanders in maintaining their language, but raises questions about the impact of colonization on Greenlandic culture and the health of the Greenlandic people.

Part III: Promising Healing Practices

Part III presents examples of healing projects in action. In this report, promising healing practices refer to models, approaches, techniques and initiatives that are based on Indigenous experience and that result in positive changes in people's lives. All of the examples have roots in Indigenous traditions, values and culture; many also include Western or mainstream practices. The examples provided are drawn from the literature reviewed for this report and the same limitations apply. Greenland, in particular, is not well represented due to the lack of published information in English.

Overall, seventeen projects and programs are profiled, including a health clinic in New Zealand that employs traditional Maori healers; traditional Navajo peacekeeping in the United States; a best practice model for addressing family violence in Australia; and a "school of life" college program in Greenland.

Conclusions: Learning Across Cultures and Nations

The experience of being colonized involves loss—of culture, language, land, resources, political autonomy, religious freedom and, often, personal autonomy. These losses may have a direct relationship to the poor health, social and economic status of Indigenous people. Understanding the need for personal and collective healing from this perspective points to a way of healing, one that combines the sociopolitical work involved in decolonization with the more personal, therapeutic healing journey.

Executive Summary

Groundbreaking research and theoretical work on treating the effects of intergenerational and historic trauma have emerged during the past decade. Such research opens the door to new approaches to healing that are especially relevant to working with survivors of residential and boarding schools. Learning about the history of colonization, mourning the losses and reconnecting with traditional cultures, values and practices are becoming recognized stages of the healing process. Indigenous people in the United States, Australia and New Zealand, as well as Canada, are all addressing historic trauma, both at a theoretical level and within therapeutic practice. This supports an early finding of the Aboriginal Healing Foundation: education about residential schools is not only an effective way to dismantle denial, but it also acts as a catalyst for individuals to engage in healing.

Secondly, cultural intervention plays a vital role in the health and healing fields. Solid arguments can be made in favour of embedding healing practices in the specific cultures, traditions and languages of Indigenous people, nations, tribes and communities. At the same time, pan-Aboriginal approaches and the sharing of Indigenous healing traditions across cultures are growing phenomena. Even ceremonies, which tend to be culturally and geographically specific, are being exchanged and shared. There is, however, a danger in assuming that healing programs working well in one context can be successfully transported to an entirely different social, cultural or political milieu. In fact, no single approach is applicable across all nations and communities.

While adaptations and sharing of Indigenous practices take place across cultures, an increased resistance to viewing Aboriginal people as having a homogeneous set of traditions and practices is evident. At a global level, efforts are required to maintain and support the cultural diversity that currently exists. At the community level, there is some evidence that culturally appropriate healing interventions are most effective when rooted in local practices, languages and traditions. At the same time, urbanization and the cumulative effects of assimilation policies have left many Indigenous people alienated from their land and culture and, sometimes, their family. Specific strategies are needed to meet the needs of Indigenous people who do not have strong cultural ties.

Finally, many healing programs incorporate, adapt and blend traditional and Western approaches. Traditional ceremonies, medicines and healing practices are being incorporated into the therapeutic process while Indigenous values and worldviews are providing the program framework. Some core values, such as holism, balance and connection to family and the environment, are common to Aboriginal worldviews across

Executive Summary

cultures; others are clearly rooted in local customs and traditions. The variety of therapeutic combinations in use suggests a powerful commitment to the values of adaptability, flexibility and innovation in the service of healing. This is consistent with the holistic approach to healing common to Indigenous value systems.

Holistic healing suggests that different therapies used in combination will more effectively address the healing needs of the whole person. For Indigenous people, the concept of holism extends beyond the mental, physical, emotional and spiritual aspects of individual lives to encompass relationships with families, communities and the physical environment. Such approaches challenge governments that compartmentalize funding through departments (health, education, housing, etc.), but they are natural to Indigenous service providers. A holistic approach also challenges many Western medical practitioners who separate physical and mental health and do not deal with the spiritual dimension.

Culturally sensitive screening and assessment tools that complement holistic and relational worldviews are required. These tools should include subject matter relevant to the people being assessed (e.g., Native American youth from a particular tribe or Maori living in a large urban centre). The subject matter should also include questions about spiritual connections, participation in ceremonies and connection to nature, culture, family and community.

In addition to the converging themes noted above, some lessons can be learned from the differences observed across cultures, nations and nation-states:

• The existence of treaties that are recognized and respected by government and incorporated into government policy, provide an environment conducive to the development of healing programs designed, delivered and controlled by Aboriginal people. This is evident in New Zealand where the *Treaty of Waitangi* is referenced in government policy.

• Failure on the part of governments to formally recognize and affirm Indigenous rights and to accept responsibility for past policies aimed at assimilating Indigenous people is an impediment to healing, both symbolically and with respect to the development of policies and programs that support individual and community healing. This is clear from the Australian experience.

Executive Summary

- Residential, boarding and mission schools in Canada, the United States and Australia shared a common goal of assimilating Indigenous children into the dominant culture and society. There are also some notable differences. In the United States, policy fluctuations in the 1930s and 1970s resulted in periods where more progressive attitudes prevailed toward Aboriginal culture, including ceremonial and religious practices. Also, the emphasis on extra-curricular activities in the American schools allowed team sports and Native American art, music, drama and dance to flourish.

- While the Canadian and Australian governments made arrangements with churches to run their institutions, most of the American schools were administered by the Bureau of Indian Affairs. A further difference is found in the accounts of former students: there are relatively fewer references to sexual abuse in American schools. While reports of sexual abuse certainly exist, the issue is not raised by former students as persistently and pervasively as in Canada or in Australia. What remains unclear is whether sexual abuse was less common in schools administered by government rather than churches or if the issue has not yet fully entered the American discourse. Further research is required to clarify this issue and to explore a possible relationship between church involvement in boarding schools and sexual abuse.

- The Western practice of documenting and evaluating therapeutic approaches and publishing the results of studies can complement traditional healing practices by providing an alternative means of knowledge transmission. This is especially effective when the researchers and authors are Indigenous people. In New Zealand, for example, an increasing number of Maori are involved in researching and writing about healing. This is not only a reflection of the growing number of Maori with professional qualifications, but also an indication that Maori knowledge about health and healing is gaining respect in its own right. The involvement of local Indigenous researchers in research and evaluation may lead to greater accountability to the community with respect to protecting traditional knowledge and following rules governing how, when and to whom it may be transmitted. Certain Western skills applied in a culturally appropriate way are especially effective if the Western-trained professional is an Aboriginal person.

In summary, a number of similarities and differences have been noted in Indigenous approaches to healing in the United States, New Zealand, Australia and Greenland. The central lesson learned about promising healing practices is the immense value and efficacy of incorporating history and culture into holistic programs based on Indigenous values and worldviews.

Introduction

In the 77 years between 1892 and 1969, generations of Aboriginal children in Canada were sent to government-sponsored residential schools run by the Roman Catholic, Anglican, United, Presbyterian and other churches. The physical and sexual abuse suffered by many of these children—along with the imposed alienation from families, communities and cultures—left scars that have been passed on from generation to generation. This legacy of abuse and intergenerational trauma is now well recognized. Sadly, Canada was not alone in its attempts to assimilate Aboriginal people through the education system. While educational policies and the criteria under which children were removed varied, many thousands of Indigenous children in the United States and Australia were taken away from their families and placed in boarding or mission schools. Colonialism took different forms in New Zealand and Greenland; if judged by the lower socioeconomic and health status of Indigenous people compared to non-Indigenous citizens, the consequences were equally damaging. This report explores colonization, decolonization and healing among Indigenous people in these four nation-states.

To establish a context for understanding decolonization, Part I provides a brief overview of Indigenous experiences under colonialism in the United States, New Zealand, Australia and Greenland, including a description of educational policies and their impact on Indigenous languages and cultures. This overview provides a backdrop for understanding the link between the experience of being colonized and the need for healing.

Part II examines recent trends in decolonization. Over the past few decades, Indigenous people across the world have been involved in movements to reassert their political and legal rights. Political development has been accompanied and supported by a renewed interest in traditional languages, ceremonies, art, music and spiritual practices. This venture into the past leads not only to a reclamation of traditional ways, but also to an examination of the policies and practices that resulted in Indigenous people's suppression. History is now being retold from an Indigenous perspective, one that details the painful losses inflicted on Indigenous societies under colonialism. Thus begins the decolonization process. New historical understandings allow people to recognize and mourn the losses experienced by past generations and then move toward a more positive, dynamic vision of the future.

Indigenous history and culture are being incorporated into healing programs in many areas of the world. In this way, decolonization is becoming a part of healing movements. Part II proposes a model of healing that blends new work by Indigenous researchers on healing from historic trauma with recent developments

Introduction

in the field of psychology for healing from post-traumatic stress. Part III presents examples of healing projects in action. Conclusions attempt to draw out common themes, as well as differences, related to the experience of colonization and decolonization.

The following is one of many definitions of healing. This definition, from a background paper prepared for the Royal Commission on Aboriginal Peoples, is put forward because it captures both the personal and the social dimensions of historical oppression and trauma:

> Healing, in Aboriginal terms, refers to personal and societal recovery from the lasting effects of oppression and systemic racism experienced over generations. Many Aboriginal people are suffering not simply from specific diseases and social problems, but also from a depression of spirit resulting from 200 or more years of damage to their cultures, languages, identities and self-respect. The idea of healing suggests that to reach 'whole health', Aboriginal people must confront the crippling injuries of the past (RCAP, 1996:109).

Methodology and Limitations

This report was conceived as an exploration of promising healing practices among Indigenous people in the United States, New Zealand, Australia and Greenland—countries with colonial histories similar, in many ways, to that of Canada. The purpose was to supplement the learning taking place about healing in Canada, especially learning that is accumulating from the national evaluations of Aboriginal Healing Foundation (AHF) program activity (Kishk Anaquot Health Research, 2001; 2002; 2003) and research into promising healing practices among AHF-funded projects. However, while doing research for this report, the focus gradually shifted away from a search for examples of healing practices that work well toward understanding the links between Indigenous experiences with colonialism, the resulting need for healing and the various approaches to healing being pursued. At this level, both similarities and differences come into clearer focus, and the report is now broader and more theoretical than first anticipated.

A full review of the literature on decolonization and healing among Indigenous people in the United States, New Zealand, Australia and Greenland is beyond the scope of this report. Rather, the analysis is based on a selection of books, journal articles, government reports and other publications available in Canada during

Introduction

the time this report was being developed. A number of sources were found electronically, especially publications from Australia, including government reports. A collection of journal articles was received from Paul Robertson of the National Addiction Centre, University of Otago in New Zealand, through the kind intervention of a colleague. Also, while in Phoenix, Arizona, on other business, the author visited the exhibition at the Heard Museum (*Remembering Our Indian School Days: The Boarding School Experience*, on exhibit from 15 November 2000 to 1 January 2006). Considerably less information was found on Greenland because so few research studies are published in English. This was confirmed by Bjerregaard and Young in their book on the health of circumpolar Inuit: "Much of the information on Greenland is only available in Danish" (1998:58).

Finally, limited information was found on Indigenous community-based healing initiatives, in part, due to the tendency of smaller projects to not publish research related to their work, no matter how innovative and successful. Knowledge within Aboriginal communities is more likely to be transmitted orally than to be included in publications available internationally. While care was taken to use reliable sources and publications, it is sometimes difficult to assess the importance of material from countries so geographically removed from Canada. However, the focus is on examining broad themes and patterns with respect to the relationship between colonization, decolonization and healing; despite limitations, the literature reviewed adequately met this purpose.

A Note on Terminology:

The terms "Indigenous" and "Aboriginal" are used interchangeably throughout this report. When discussing Aboriginal people living in a particular nation-state, an attempt is made to use more specific terms. Literature in the United States uses the terms "Indian," "American Indian" and "Native American;" the names of specific tribes (i.e., Apache, Assiniboine, Choctaw, Oregon, Lakota, etc.) are used whenever that information is available. The American literature refers to Inuit as "Eskimo." The term "Aboriginal and Torres Strait Islanders" is used in Australia. The Indigenous people of New Zealand are Maori. In Greenland, the terms "Inuit" or "Greenlander" are used.

Part I

An Overview of Colonization

Poka Laenui (2000), an Indigenous Hawaiian, describes colonization and decolonization[1] as being social processes, each characterized by five distinct but interconnected phases. Interestingly, the phases of decolonization, discussed in Part II, share similarities with what are now well-recognized steps in the process of healing from post-traumatic stress. Laenui's phases of colonization are summarized below:

- Denial and withdrawal: The colonial culture is viewed as the only real culture. Colonial people deny the value and even the existence of Indigenous culture. Indigenous people gradually withdraw from their own cultural practices.

- Destruction/eradication of all physical symbols of Indigenous culture; destruction of sacred sites, art and ceremonial objects.

- Denigration/belittlement/insult: Colonial institutions (church, health and legal systems) denigrate and belittle Indigenous systems and any continuing practice of the Indigenous culture. For example, Aboriginal belief systems and ceremonies may be characterized as devil worship and traditional healers as witch doctors. Some traditional practices may be criminalized.

- Surface accommodation/tokenism: In this phase, the remnants of Indigenous culture are tolerated as folklore and given token regard.

- Transformation/exploitation: Aspects of traditional culture that refuse to disappear are transformed into the culture of the colonial society. Examples include: Christian churches using Aboriginal pastors or priests and permitting the use of Aboriginal languages; economically exploiting Indigenous art; and using traditional symbols and designs to decorate clothing and buildings.

Various characteristics and permutations of these phases of colonization can be recognized in the history of the United States, New Zealand, Australia and Greenland—although not necessarily chronologically and not all phases are evident in every country. Table 1 provides an overview of critical events in the colonial history of each nation-state. This is followed by a description of the colonization process in each country.

---

[1]   Laenui credits these observations on colonization and decolonization to the late Virgilio Enriques.

Part I

Table 1) Overview of Colonization in the United States, New Zealand, Australia and Greenland*

Nation-State	Indigenous Population	Colonizer	Treaties	Residential/Boarding Schools	Role of Churches	Colonial Legislation/Policy	Recognition of Historic Injustice
United States	+ 700 tribes; 4.1 million Native Americans, including Alaskan Natives; 1.5 per cent of total population (2000)	Spain, England, France; after 1776, the United States	Yes, some treaties pre-1871; almost constant warfare until 1890	Missionaries established schools in 17th century; first government-run off-reservation boarding school established in 1879	Some mission schools, especially in early years, but primarily government-run boarding schools	1871 *Indian Appropriation Act* withdrew constitutional recognition of tribes as sovereign nations; 1887 *Allotment Act* privatized tribal lands	No formal apology; Meriam Report (1928) and Kennedy Report (1969) condemned boarding school policy
New Zealand	Maori: 255,000 (2001) or 15 per cent of New Zealand's population	England	Yes. Treaty of Waitangi, 1840; New Zealand Wars, 1845 to 1872: Maori resist confiscation of land	No, church-run community schools	Primarily Catholic and some Anglican churches ran community schools	1858 *Native Schools Act* required schools to teach in English; 1907 *Tohunga Suppression Act*; Maori relocated from traditional lands (50 per cent now live in cities)	Government recognition and incorporation of Maori healing in health system; Maori an official language
Australia	Aboriginal and Torres Strait Islanders: 410,003 (2001 Census): 2.2 per cent of population	England	No	Yes, beginning in early 1900s; children of mixed parents especially vulnerable	Church-run boarding schools, missions	1911: Chief Protectors given power over Indigenous people; removal from traditional to reserved lands	No apology from federal government; yes, from states and territories; Sorry Day; National Inquiry—*Bringing Them Home* report (1997)
Greenland	Population of 56,000 (1999); 90 per cent identify as ethnic Greenlanders (or 80 per cent Inuit)	Denmark	No, but also no private ownership of land	No, public school system (day schools); Danish system duplicated in Greenland	Lutheran missionaries established missions and schools in 1700s	No wars, no private land ownership; Denmark-owned mineral rights until 1979; Danish-style government administration and school system	1979: Greenland achieved Home Rule

* Population figures for the United States, New Zealand and Australia are based on census data. Measurement techniques and tools vary across countries, so making comparisons may not be reliable. For example, numbers may vary depending on whether the census counts Indigenous persons by self-identity or by ancestry. Furthermore, Indigenous organizations within each country may not agree with the census figures. Greenland's population was reported in the International Journal of Circumpolar Health (Bjerregaard et. al. 2003).

Part I

United States

According to the United States Census 2000, 1.5 per cent of the population is American Indian and Alaska Native (4.1 million out of a total population of 281.4 million). The federal government currently recognizes 561 tribes; many others are not officially recognized. Federally-recognized tribes are entitled to health and educational services provided by the federal government. Over half of Native Americans do not live on reservations and, therefore, have no access to federally-funded health services. Over 200 Indigenous languages are spoken and each tribe has its own distinct culture, beliefs and practices. The most populous tribes (+50,000 individuals in 2000) are Cherokee, Navajo, Latin American Indian, Choctaw, Sioux, Chippewa, Apache, Blackfeet, Iroquois and Pueblo (Ogunwole, 2002). The Indigenous population of Alaska includes Tlingit-Haida, Athabascan, Inuit (Inupiat) and Aleut. Of this group, the Inuit are the most populous: "There were 45,919 respondents who reported Eskimo alone and an additional 8,842 who reported Eskimo with at least one other race or American Indian or Alaska Native tribal grouping" (Ogunwole, 2002:9).[2]

The Office of the Surgeon General reports that Native Americans experience higher rates of poverty, unemployment, homelessness, suicide, violent victimization, post-traumatic stress and incarceration than non-Native Americans. Prior to the 1978 *Indian Child Welfare Act*, an estimated 25 to 30 per cent of Native American children had been removed from their families (United States Department of Health and Human Services, 1999).

Historical Overview

From the 1600s on, the territories of Indigenous tribes in North America were being invaded by the English, Spanish and French and, later, by the Americans. History records the Pequot War, 1637; Iroquois War, 1642 to 1653; King William's War 1689 to 1697; Pontiac's War, 1763 to 1766; Creek War, 1813 to 1814; First Seminole War, 1817 to 1818; Second Seminole War, 1835 to 1842; and so on. In some cases, tribes were directly attacked; in others, they were drawn into a round-robin of revolving alliances as England, Spain and France fought over pieces of North America.[3] From the 1776 American Revolution until 1871, Native American tribes were recognized as sovereign nations in the American constitution. The *Indian Appropriation Act* of 1871

---

[2]   In literature originating in the United States, the Inuit are referred to as Eskimo.
[3]   See Angie Debo's *A History of the Indians of the United States* (1983) for a detailed historical review of the colonization of the United States from the 1400s on.

Part I

withdrew this recognition. Signed treaties remained in force until these were superseded by Congress. Then, under the *General Allotment Act* (1887), tribal lands were divided into small, individually-owned parcels of land. Tribes owned 140 million acres of land in 1887, but less than 50 million acres in 1934 (Health Canada, 2001).

Spanish and English missionaries began establishing missions and schools in the 1600s. Converting Native North Americans to Christianity was a high priority. For example, English Pastor John Eliot took Pequot captives into his family so that he could learn to speak the local Algonquian dialect and could more effectively preach. "He helped his converts form Christian villages ... started churches and schools in the villages and made preachers and teachers of his converts.... By 1674 there were two established Indian churches, fourteen Indian towns, and 1,100 "Praying Indians" " (Debo, 1983:47). A federal school system for Native Americans was not established until almost two hundred years later in the 1860s. In 1879, the first off-reservation boarding school was opened in Carlisle, Pennsylvania (Archuleta et. al., 2000). An army officer who believed education was the key to "civilizing" Indian children established the school. The federal superintendent of Indian schools in 1885 saw his task as "making the Indian "a member of a new social order," envisioned it thus: "we must recreate him, make him a new personality"" (Debo,1983:287).

There were 25 off-reservation industrial boarding schools operating by 1900. The first students were primarily Lakota, forcibly taken from their families as hostages to "guarantee their parents' and communities' 'good behavior' and cooperation with federal agents" (Archuleta et. al., 2000:14). The boarding schools were decidedly militaristic: students were separated by age and gender; the boys wore military-style uniforms and participated in routine drills, parades and inspections; and strict, military-style regimentation and discipline were the norm.

Students living in cramped residences were exposed to disease (trachoma, influenza, tuberculosis) and undernourishment. Funding was generally at such a low level that student labour was necessary to run the schools (Archuleta et. al., 2000). The daily program included growing food, tending cattle, sewing clothing, washing and ironing clothing and linen, cooking, cleaning, and other agricultural or domestic duties. Vocational training was an important part of the school curriculum; for example, boys at the Phoenix Indian School, which opened in 1891 in Phoenix, Arizona, could learn masonry, carpentry, painting, plumbing, electrical work, auto mechanics, shoemaking, tailoring or banking, as well as agriculture and animal husbandry. The school included a farming operation and both male and female students worked on the farm (Parker, 1996). Girls were also taught domestic skills such as child rearing, sewing, preparing food and home nursing.

Part I

Adolescents attending boarding schools were placed in non-Native households to work as farm hands and domestic servants during holidays. This was known as the "outing" program. Association with non-Native people was considered a "civilizing" influence.

While a standardized curriculum known as the *Uniform Course of Study for Indian Schools in the United States* was in effect until the 1930s, "teachers in Indian schools have struggled with poor materials or no materials at all, devised their own courses, and patched together curricula" (Archuleta et. al., 2000:33). Whatever the resources, the underlying purpose of the educational process remained constant over time:

> These efforts have been united across generations by four commonalities: their intent to eradicate Native languages (despite some sporadic attempts in the 1930s to introduce bilingual materials, particularly in the Southwest); their concentration on the basics of the "Three Rs" (reading, writing, and 'rithmetic); their assumption that Indians would not aspire to or be fitted for higher education or professional training; and their emphasis on "practical" education (Archuleta et. al., 2000:33).

In 1930, almost 90 per cent of Native American children were enrolled in school—approximately half in public school, over a third in schools operated by the Indian Bureau, and almost ten per cent in private or mission schools.[4] "Of those who attended Indian Bureau schools, an equal number were enrolled in off-reservation and reservation boarding schools and a much smaller percentage were in day schools" (Szasz, 1999:2). Many American public schools would not enrol Indian children until after World War II; as public schooling became accessible, boarding school attendance dropped. Schools responded by recruiting students from more remote areas of the country.

The Ebb and Flow of Government Policy

In 1926, the federal government asked the Institute for Government Research to undertake a survey of social and economic conditions of Indians throughout the United States. *The Problem of Indian Administration,*

---

[4]   Szasz (1999:271), footnote 13: In 1930, 72,000 Indian children were in school; of these, approximately 6,000 or 8.3 per cent attended mission schools. In 1969, there were 178,000 Indian children in school—10,500 or 6 per cent attended "mission or other schools" (i.e., not Bureau of Indian Affairs or public schools). Mission schools, some of which opened in the seventeenth century, were subsidized by the federal government from 1810 to 1917.

Part I

referred to as the Meriam Report, was issued in 1928 and it radically altered the overt policy goal of assimilation, at least for a time. In the Meriam Report, the allotment policy was a particular focus of criticism. Allotment was the process whereby individual members of a tribe could select a piece of farmland (an allotment) and become a citizen of the state. It was used as a means of opening up tribal lands for white settlement and liquidating the tribe. In many cases, allotment proceeded without the consent of the individuals or tribes involved. The Meriam Report stated:

> For forty years, as tribe after tribe was liquidated and thousands upon thousands of individuals entered, in theory, the general pattern of white life and culture, it had all been reported in terms of "progress." Now for the first time deplorable conditions of poverty, disease, lack of social and economic adjustment, suffering, and discontent were uncovered, and the allotment policy was cited as the main cause. "The strength of the ancient system of communal ownership was not realized" was the conclusion (Debo, 1983:336).

Meriam recommended that education become the primary function of the Indian Bureau[5] and that a number of changes be made. These changes included bringing education closer to the community, constructing day schools that would also serve as community centres and introducing Indian culture into the curriculum. The report attacked the physical conditions of boarding schools, the enrolment of preadolescent children and the inadequacy of the personnel (Szasz, 1999). This both reflected and ushered in a new era based on the principles of the progressive education movement that were popular at the time. Applied to Indian education, progressive education allowed for the inclusion of cross-cultural components, such as local customs, practices, art, music and even religion (Szasz, 1999). The years between 1930 and 1945, known as the *Indian New Deal*, saw a shift away from the goal of assimilation and toward a recognition and respect for tribal cultures: "the BIA changed course in policy, seeming to turn the tide against federal suppression of Indian arts and traditions" (Green and Troutman, 2000:77).

Even during this progressive period, support for reform at the BIA level did not necessarily translate into changes on the ground. Resistance by many bureaucrats, school administrators and teachers who remained committed to assimilationist policies continued. Moreover, plans to gradually phase out boarding schools proved difficult to implement. From 1928 to 1933, the number of boarding schools dropped from 77 to 65;

---

[5]   The Indian Bureau is now called the Bureau of Indian Affairs (BIA).

Part I

some changed to day schools and children in lower grades were being transferred to on-reserve day schools and, sometimes, public schools (Szasz, 1999). Yet, overall, the number of children in boarding schools was greater in 1933 than in 1928, partly due to a lack of funding to construct new day schools and partly because the Native American population was growing: "by 1941 there were still forty-nine boarding schools with a total enrollment of about 14,000 children" (Szasz, 1999:60). The tide turned once again toward assimilation after World War II. Under the *1953 Termination Policy*, tribes were directed to distribute property to their members and to dissolve their governments. At the same time, *Public Law 280* extended the jurisdiction of state governments with respect to civil and criminal law to Indian reservations (Debo, 1983).

In 1969, a second study on Indian conditions brought boarding schools to the attention of policy makers, politicians and the American public. The Kennedy Report, *A National Tragedy–A National Challenge: Report of the Committee on Labor and Public Welfare, Special Sub-committee on Indian Education*, stated that conditions had not changed since the Meriam Report and that many of its recommendations had not been implemented. Evidence of any advances made during the 1930s had disappeared in subsequent decades and the Kennedy Report attacked the "disastrous effects" of the coercive policy of assimilation (Szasz, 1999). In 1970, the American government issued its Indian self-determination policy and reaffirmed the special legal status of Indians. This led to the *Indian Self-Determination and Education Assistance Act*, 1975. However, state governments retain enough authority that the implementation of self-determination varies across the country (Health Canada, 2001).

Boarding School Experiences and Impacts

An exhibition at the Heard Museum in Phoenix, Arizona, *Remembering Our Indian School Days: The Boarding School Experience*, and the accompanying publication explore the experiences of former students and speak eloquently of the pervasiveness of assimilation through education. Yet, in spite of goals to eradicate "Indianness," attendance at boarding schools sometimes resulted in increased pride and a strong sense of identity. A statement on the walls of the museum's boarding school exhibition asserted that the schools were designed to change the Indian into a "white man," but instead, the students changed the schools into "Indian" schools. "In so many ways, Native students turned attempts to repress and replace Native tradition into something viable and vital, for themselves as individuals and for their Native communities, local and national" (Green and Troutman, 2000:83). It is also true that overt efforts to assimilate Aboriginal children waxed and waned over the years (in contrast to Canada) and individual students reacted to or against assimilation in a wide variety of ways. There were acts of resistance and rebellion, but lifelong friendships were also forged. From time to time, federal policies supported the inclusion of traditional arts and culture in the curriculum (Archuleta et. al., 2000).

Even during the most repressive periods, boarding school students participated in a wide variety of extra-curricular activities, including organized sports, drama and instruction in music and art. Over time, activities included Indian clubs and Indian dance clubs,[6] which revolved around traditional music and dancing and the making and wearing of traditional clothing. Traditional art and design were also taught in a number of the schools.[7] Beginning in 1932, the Santa Fe Indian School in New Mexico operated as an arts and crafts centre for the Indian boarding school system and the program was recognized by government as having good economic potential.

Students survived the boarding school experience by drawing upon a wealth of personal and collective strategies and strengths: "strategies of human survival—resistance, accommodation, faith in oneself and one's heritage, the ability to learn from hard times, to create something beautiful and meaningful from scraps and fragments" (Archuleta, et. al., 2000:19). The stories told by survivors included many of the now-familiar horrors recounted by former residential school students in Canada—physical abuse, corporal punishment, racism, forced assimilation (including adopting English names and prohibitions against speaking their language), forced removal from family and community, and immersion in 'white' culture.

Federal Indian boarding schools included students from diverse geographic regions, nations and tribes. In addition to assimilation, another goal was to alienate children from their tribal identity: "They were designed to obliterate tribal identity, to destroy Native languages, to eradicate Native religions" (Buffalohead and Molin, 2000:116). While there is evidence that some parents freely chose to send their children to school, resistance is also well documented. For example, in 1895, Chief Lomahognyoma and 18 other Hopi men were

---

[6] Traditional music and dance were controversial because they were associated with traditional religious ceremonies and churches were especially opposed. Government officials were also concerned and, in 1923, the Commissioner of Indian Affairs issued a letter "To All Indians" forbidding most dances on reservations unless approved by reservation superintendents (Archuleta et. al., 2000). Despite this, many BIA boarding schools had Indian dance clubs that performed at fairs and other events in nearby communities.

[7] For example, Ho Chunk (Winnebego) artist Angel de Cora taught art at Carlisle for nine years ending in 1915. She was a classically-trained artist who grew up attending Hampton Boarding School, then continued her education at Smith College, Cowles Art School and the Boston Museum of Fine Arts. Her teaching was inspired through travel to a number of reservations where she observed women's cultural lives, including weaving, pottery and appliqué. She also studied a variety of tribal designs. The art program ended when she left Carlisle in 1915, but was reinstated in the 1930s (Archuleta et. al., 2000).

Part I

incarcerated at Alcatraz for acts of resistance that included refusing to send their children to federal schools (Archuleta, et. al., 2000).

With respect to physical abuse, the literature is very clear. The Heard Museum's publication includes the following account of physical abuse:

> Violence, abuse and neglect stemmed from the boarding schools' entrenched commitment to erasing Indian identity. Not only were children removed from their parents, often forcibly, but they had their mouths washed out with lye soap when they spoke their Native languages; they could be locked up in the guardhouse with only bread and water for other rule violations; and they faced corporal punishment and other rigid discipline on a daily basis. In addition to these intentional practices, schools also fostered more insidious violence: gang warfare between tribes, the "belt lines" boys had to run, and the sadism of dormitory advisors or "disciplinarians" (Archuleta et. al., 2000:42).

Stories of sexual abuse are less frequently told. The publication mentions Canadian court cases and the Canadian government's 1998 *Statement of Reconciliation*, but reported that these issues have remained more private in the United States, "as individuals, families and communities struggle with the darker legacies of boarding school life" (Archeluta et. al., 2000:43). What remains unclear is whether the incidence of sexual abuse was lower in United States boarding schools than in the predominantly church-run residential schools in Canada or if the issue of sexual abuse has not yet fully entered the public discourse.

The off-reservation boarding school system in the United States was similar to Canada's residential school system to the extent that the overriding goal was to assimilate Aboriginal children into the dominant society and culture. A number of differences are also evident. The majority of off-reservation boarding schools in the United States were run by government, not churches. As well, there were short periods of time in American history where Aboriginal cultures were allowed to flourish in the schools. Another difference was the emphasis on extra-curricular activities in the American schools, including team sports, art, music, drama, dance and Indian clubs. There has been no mention of an official government apology for the abuses that occurred in the boarding school system. However, twice in the last century, influential reports[8] to government have exposed the disastrous consequences of Indian education policy in the United States.

---

[8]   The Meriam Report in 1928 and the Kennedy Report in 1969.

Part I

New Zealand (Aotearoa[9])

Approximately fifteen per cent of the four million people living in New Zealand are Maori. They are overrepresented in jails,[10] their socioeconomic and health status lag behind that of the non-Maori or *Paheka* population, and Maori youth suicide rates are higher compared to non-Maori youth[11] (Coupe, 2000). A government program, *Closing the Gaps*, announced in the 2000 Budget, included the goal of reducing disparities between Maori and non-Maori.[12]

Issues of Maori identity are sometimes controversial, since many people have both Maori and *Paheka* ancestors. Novelist Witi Ihimaera calls the notion of Maori identity problematic and claims there is no racial or full-blooded definition. Rather, people make a sovereign choice to identify, "based on genealogy, belonging, upbringing, pride, politics or downright stubbornness that links them with the mana of our Maori forbears - the ancestors in front and we behind" (Ihimaera, 1998:14). Other definitions focus on self-identification and participation in various aspects of Maori culture (Huriwai et. al., 2001).

Historical Overview

When Captain Cook "discovered" Aotearoa in 1769, more than a thousand years had passed since Maori had settled the islands. The *Treaty of Waitangi* was signed on February 6, 1840. The treaty was written in English and Maori; however, since the two versions vary, Maori and government interpretations differ. The treaty was viewed by the colonizers as establishing British sovereignty over New Zealand and, by Maori, as guaranteeing their sovereignty and protecting their lands. In spite of the treaty, the colonial government confiscated Maori lands and undermined the economic base, culture and language. Resistance to the large-scale confiscation of land resulted in the "New Zealand Wars" (1845-1872). The eventual defeat of the Maori has been attributed to the superior weapons of the British troops and the continued influx of settlers (Jones, 2000b). By the late nineteenth century, large numbers of Maori had been relocated from hilltop land to coastal areas, geographically removing them from

---

[9]   Maori words are commonly used in publications and articles, even those published by the New Zealand government. Some of these words have been used in this section, although the proper accents are, unfortunately, missing from this text. This is a technical issue and no disrespect for the Maori language is intended.

[10]   Huriwai and colleagues (2001) report that Maori constitute 52 per cent of the prison population.

[11]   In 1997, Maori rate of suicide was 17.5/100,000 compared to 13.1/100,000 for non-Maori (Coupe, 2000).

[12]   Programs that focus on reducing the disparities between Maori and non-Maori segments of the population have been criticized for their inability to address deep-rooted development issues and the risk that policies will be formulated on the basis of Maori being a marginalized minority (Durie, 2000). Others caution that a focus on disparity alone is inadequate: there must also be a parallel focus on Maori health development and addressing societal drivers, especially racism (Reid et. al., 2000).

traditional food supplies. Alienation from traditional lands continued into the twentieth century as more and more people moved into cities. Ihimaera wrote about this stage of Maori history in his introduction to a collection of essays entitled *Growing up Māori*:

> The post-war years accelerated this great rural to urban drift and the accompanying discontinuity in transmission of Māori family histories and culture across time and space. By the 1950s, at least fifty percent of Māori lived in urban areas. By far the greatest challenges to Māori have been in how they have managed the journey (Ihimaera, 1998:13).

War, relocation and the introduction of infectious diseases resulted in a serious decline in the Maori population. Estimates range from between 100,000 and 115,000 prior to European contact to approximately 42,000 by 1896 (Jones, 2000b). Soldiers returning from World War I brought a flu virus that resulted in another wave of sickness and death. Mihi Edwards, a Maori Elder born in 1911, remembered how ineffective traditional medicine was in dealing with this new virus: "There was a plant for everything - infections, infected sores, sterilising, stomach upsets, blood poisoning, poultices - everything.... But they had no medicine for this flu. ...They couldn't cope with it" (Ihimaera, 1998:98-99).

The *Native Schools Act, 1858* established subsidies for Maori education in missionary schools. To obtain government subsidies, schools were required to teach in English. In 1867, an extension of the act offered village schools to Maori communities: in return for providing land, the community received a school, teacher and books. Agreements were reached with religious groups, mainly Catholic, who received the land in exchange for building and operating community schools. With increased urbanization, many Maori attended school in the city where their history, language and culture were either ignored or suppressed. Children were expected to become part of a modern, mainstream society. In the 1990s, *Kura Kaupapa* Maori schools sprang up across New Zealand as a response to the loss of language and culture and they offered Maori children a total immersion experience. These are private day or boarding schools run by and for Maori. In May 2000, a government press release announced funding for a number of these schools: "Thirty-two Kura Kaupapa Maori, Maori Boarding schools, Wharekura and other schools that use Maori language as the primary source of instruction now qualify for funding as part of the government's Gateway programme for schools" (Horomia, 2003).

Part I

Traditional Maori Healing

The *whanau* or extended family is the central social unit and often includes three or more generations. A number of families make up a *hapu* or sub-tribe and the largest entity is known as the *iwi*. Each *iwi* is considered a nation in its own right. Traditionally, there were three classes of citizens—chiefs, commoners and slaves—and individuals were born into a particular rank. There was also a second class of leader, the *tohunga*, which included political leaders as well as artists (carvers, canoe-builders, tattooists, house builders), experts in agriculture, fishing, warfare and healing. Some *tohunga* trained for as long as seven years, learning astrology, genealogy, faith healing, special incantations and tribal history (Jones, 2000b). Today, the word *tohunga* is most commonly used to refer to traditional healers.

The Maori worldview is holistic and encompasses four qualities: spirit and soul, thoughts and feelings, the physical body, and the extended family. In a thesis examining the issues involved in incorporating traditional healing into the New Zealand public health system, Rhys Jones (2000b) describes traditional Maori healing.[13]

Traditionally, Maori had a strong spiritual connection to the earth and illness was viewed as a symptom of imbalance or disharmony with nature. Malignant spirits were thought to bring on illness, often in response to the breaking of a taboo. A traditional healer would deal with the situation first by gathering a thorough case history of all the patient's actions prior to the illness, a process that might include analysis of the patient's dreams. Once the spirit was identified, the healer would appeal to it to leave the patient. A purification ritual would follow. If sorcery was identified as the cause of the illness, the healer would attempt to turn the spell back on the perpetrator. If the treatment was successful, the sorcerer died; if not, the patient died. For everyday illnesses and injuries, treatment involved herbal medicines, minor surgery and a form of massage. Maori medicines proved ineffective against newly-introduced infectious diseases, such as measles and influenza. Missionaries, who were familiar with the course of these diseases and had access to Western medicines, played a significant role in undermining Maori beliefs, traditions and medicines and, with them, the status of traditional healers (Jones, 2000b):

> Given the apparent impotence of their own healers, many Māori ... turned to Christianity.
> The effect of this was that Māori, perhaps for the first time as a people, began to question their

---

[13]   Jones reports that the practice of *rongoa Maori* (traditional healing) in precolonial times is the subject of considerable debate, since available evidence is based on oral histories and the work of early anthropologists (Jones, 2000b).

faith in their own gods. Since their religion was inextricably bound up with their culture and everyday life, there were wider ramifications in terms of dissolution of their Māori identity (Jones, 2000b:30).

In 1900, the *Maori Councils Act* included provisions for traditional healers or *tohunga* with expertise in herbal medicine to register with the newly-formed Maori Councils. This was an attempt to distinguish between these healers and a group of faith healers considered to be swindlers and quacks. The regulation process did not appear to work. In 1907, the *Tohunga Suppression Act* made it illegal to use any type of sorcery or enchantment or to claim to have supernatural powers in the treatment of disease. Jones called the act "a direct challenge to Māori healing practices by the scientific medical establishment" (2000b:32). This led to many of the healers being driven underground. In the end, not many Maori were charged because officials found it difficult to find anyone who would testify against a *tohunga*, "largely due to the unshakable faith that the majority of Māori people had retained in their own healers" (Jones, 2000b:33). The act was repealed in 1962. Today, traditional Maori healing is a recognized part of New Zealand's formal health care system. In 1999, the Ministry of Health published standards of practice for traditional Maori healing.

Australia

The 2001 Census reported 18,972,350 people living in Australia, of which 410,003 (2.2 per cent) identified as being of Indigenous origin. Almost half (42 per cent) of Aboriginal people live in towns and small urban centres with populations between 1,000 and 99,000; 27 per cent live in rural and remote areas; and 31 per cent live in cities with populations over 100,000 (Fryer-Smith, 2002). Yet, the country itself is highly urbanized, with almost two-thirds of the total population living in cities with over 100,000 residents. Approximately two-thirds of the hundreds of original Aboriginal languages are extinct or nearly extinct, and only 20 of the 90 surviving languages are classified as healthy (Fryer-Smith, 2002). On a more optimistic note, a 1994 survey reported that 68 per cent of Indigenous youth had attended a cultural event in the past twelve months and almost one in five spoke an Aboriginal or Torres Strait Islander language—in rural areas, the rate of language use rose to 42 per cent (Australia HREOC, 1997).

Social statistics and health status are truly alarming. Indigenous Australians are 45 times more likely to be a victim of domestic violence than other Australians, 8.1 times more likely to be homicide victims, and 16.6 per cent more likely to commit homicide. They experience higher rates of self-injury, suicide and incarceration—15 times the rate of other Australians (Reconciliation Australia, 2002). The mortality rate of Aboriginal and Torres Strait Islander people is twice as high as the Maori, 2.3 times the rate of Indigenous people in the United States, and 3.1 times the total Australian rate (Australian National Audit Office, 2002).

Historical Overview

Aboriginal people are believed to have migrated to Australia between 50,000 and 60,000 years ago. In 1770, Captain Cook claimed eastern Australia for Britain and, in 1788, the first settlement was established as a penal colony. For the next half century, British convicts were shipped to Australia to be used as free labour on the sheep farms being established by other British settlers. Australia is the only commonwealth country that did not sign a formal treaty with the original inhabitants. In fact, it was not until the High Court's 1992 *Mabo* decision that Native title was recognized. Until then, the predominant legal and political doctrine was based on a view of the land as essentially unoccupied (*terra nullius*) prior to British settlement. This suggests an extremely hostile political environment where, until very recently, Aboriginal people had few legal rights. The *Native Titles Act, 1993* led to over one thousand agreements being reached; however, unlike land claims settlements in Canada, parties to agreements include private enterprises as well as government bodies.

Beginning in the early 1900s, Aboriginal children in Australia were removed from their families and placed in non-Aboriginal foster homes or institutions. These children are referred to as members of the "stolen generations." Children with light-coloured skin were most vulnerable. Professor Lowitja O'Donoghue, in a keynote address to the 2001 'Healing the Pain' Stolen Generations Conference, said:

> The attitudes and policies of the time—which were supported by the legal system as well as by influential members of the Church, meant that children of mixed parentage were removed. The thinking behind this was, that the older and traditional Aboriginal people would die out and that the so-called half castes (assisted by their white genes), would become integrated into the white industrial classes (2001:106).

Beginning in 1911, all states, except Tasmania, appointed a "Chief Protector" or a "Protection Board" with powers over Indigenous people. People needed permission to leave the reserve, to marry or to get a job. Parents lost all decision-making power over their children. In some states, the chief protector was made legal guardian

Part I

of all Aboriginal children (Gannage, 1998). During this period, Aboriginal people were also being systematically removed from their traditional lands to "reserved" lands. No treaties were signed. "The management of the reserves was delegated to government appointed managers or missionaries in receipt of government subsidies. Enforcement of the protectionist legislation at the local level was the responsibility of 'protectors' who were usually police officers" (Australia HREOC, 1997: Part 2, Chapter 2). Many of the children sent to church-run schools never saw their parents again. The Human Rights and Equal Opportunity Commission (HREOC), in its groundbreaking report, *Bringing Them Home: Report of the National Inquiry into the Separation of Aboriginal and Torres Strait Islander Children from Their Families* (Australia HREOC, 1997) was unable to state how many children were forcibly removed due to the inadequacy of available records. However, some estimates were ventured:

> Nationally we can conclude with confidence that between one in three and one in ten Indigenous children were forcibly removed from their families and communities in the period from approximately 1910 until 1970. In certain regions and in certain periods the figure was undoubtedly much greater than one in ten. In that time not one Indigenous family has escaped the effects of forcible removal (confirmed by representatives of the Queensland and WA [Western Australia] Governments in evidence to the Inquiry). Most families have been affected, in one or more generations, by the forcible removal of one or more children (1997: Part 2, Chapter 2).

The report concludes that churches shared some responsibility for forcible removals because of their involvement in providing accommodation, education, training and work placements for the children.[14]

Bringing Them Home reports that children, especially girls, were vulnerable to sexual abuse and exploitation in institutions, foster homes and job placements. The following rates of sexual abuse are based on the testimony of Commission witnesses:[15]

---

[14]   "The Aboriginal Legal Service of WA [Western Australia] advised the Inquiry that 85% of the people it interviewed who had been forcibly removed as children had spent at least part of their childhood in the care of a mission. Nationally the proportion is probably somewhat lower" (Australia HREOC, 1997: Part 5, Chapter 19).

[15]   Witnesses were not asked whether they had experienced sexual abuse and there are many reasons, personal and procedural, for deciding against volunteering the information.

- almost one in ten boys and just over one in ten girls alleged they were sexually abused in a children's institution;

- one in ten boys and three in ten girls alleged they were sexually abused in a foster placement or placements; and

- one in ten girls alleged they were sexually abused in a work placement organized by the Protection Board or institution (Australia HREOC, 1997).

By 1940, the New South Wales Board's poor record with respect to Aborigine girls placed in service was well known and even condemned in parliament. In spite of this knowledge, the board was not abolished until 1969. However, the removal of Indigenous children continued:

> A high proportion of people affected by the past laws, practices and policies of forcible removal have had their own children taken from them in turn. The ALSWA [Aboriginal Legal Service of Western Australia] survey of 483 clients who were removed in childhood revealed that more than one-third (35.2%) had had their children removed ... A process of second (or subsequent) generation removal occurred in more than one in three cases (Australia HREOC, 1997: Part 6, Chapter 20).

In a paper prepared for the Law Commission of Canada, Mark Gannage (1998) asserts the number of stolen children actually increased during the 1950s and 1960s. At the same time, it was becoming clear that the assimilation policy was not working. In 1967, the goal of assimilation was replaced with integration and, during the 1970s, the Labor Party was elected on a platform that included Aboriginal self-determination. After the election, Aboriginal groups began to have access to government funding that allowed them to challenge the removal of children. As a result, the numbers began to decline. However, it was not until the 1980s when policies changed to ensure that, when Aboriginal and Torres Strait Islander children were to be placed in out-of-home care, they should be placed within their own culture and community. In 1995, the Attorney-General of Australia asked the Human Rights and Equal Opportunity Commission to inquire into, and report on, removal of children from their families, including tracing past laws and policies and examining the adequacy and need for changes in current laws, practices and policies. This led to the *Bringing Them Home* report mentioned above.

Part I

Bringing Them Home recognizes the loss, grief and trauma experienced by Aboriginal people across generations. The report documents psychological, physical and sexual abuse, sexual exploitation, racism, intergenerational trauma and loss of Aboriginal identity, culture, heritage and community and spiritual connections. The report recognizes the importance of testimony. The first of fifty-four recommendations states funding should be made available to Indigenous agencies to record, preserve and administer a process of testimony of people affected by the forcible removal policies. *Bringing Them Home* also recommended the establishment of a national Aboriginal oral history archive and that the government acknowledge and formally apologize for the removals.

Greenland

Greenland's 1995 population was 55,732; 87 per cent were born in Greenland. The term "Greenlander" is used for people born in Greenland; of the remaining residents, most were born in Denmark. The majority of Greenlanders are Inuit, followed by people of Danish and mixed ancestries. The Inuit population is divided between Nuuk with an estimated population of 13,000 of which 9,500 are Inuit, and 16 other small towns and 60 villages. Nuuk is a Westernized, urban centre. The traditional Inuit lifestyle is more predominant in the northern villages.[16] Access to health services and the health status of the population vary with geography. In general, health status and living conditions are poorer in the villages than in towns. There are no roads linking towns and villages. Travel is primarily by boat and, in the northern areas, dog sled. Medical evacuations take place primarily by helicopter as the terrain will not accommodate air strips. Without runways, medical evacuations are dependent upon good weather conditions and, as a result, community health professionals are required to deal with more emergency procedures than in isolated regions of Canada. Finally, the majority of doctors and nurses are Danish professionals who come to Greenland for short-term assignments, and few of these Danish physicians speak Greenlandic. In 1996, a nursing school opened in Nuuk in an attempt to increase the number of Greenlanders working in the health field (Bjerregaard and Young, 1998).

Greenlanders experience lower levels of health than their counterparts in Denmark. Child mortality rates were five times higher in Greenland than in Denmark, and mortality rates among the 15 to 44 age group were four times higher. Greenlanders have a lower overall life expectancy, as well as higher infant mortality rates (infant mortality is higher in Greenland than among Canadian and Alaskan Inuit). For Inuit in Greenland, 27 per

---

[16]   The population and health data and the health system information presented in this section are based on Bjerregaard and Young (1998). This book is one of the few English sources of health information on Inuit in Greenland.

cent of all deaths were due to injuries, including accidents, suicides and homicides; 14 per cent due to cancers; and 11 per cent to lung disease. "Suicides and alcohol abuse are some extreme indicators of poor mental health. Among the 18-34 age group, 19% of men and 24% of women have thought seriously of committing suicide, while 49% in all age groups combined have experienced suicide in a relative or close friend" (Bjerregaard and Young, 1998:53).

Greenlandic (or Kalaallisut), a dialect of Inuktitut, is the official language as well as the first language of most of the population. Ninety-seven per cent speak Greenlandic (Bjerregaard and Young, 1998); it is the primary language of education, of many published books and newspapers and of radio and television programs. The traditional economy was based on hunting (sea mammals and birds) and fishing, but hunting in the past 50 years has become insufficient to satisfy the economic needs of Inuit (Leineweber and Arensman, 2003). The economy suffered from the effects of the European ban on sealskins, as well as reductions in cod and shrimp stocks, during the 1980s. While cryolite was mined between 1850 and the 1980s, the economic benefits accrued mainly to Denmark (Petersen, 1995). Tourism and administration are significant segments of the current economy.

Historical Overview

Greenland was colonized by Denmark in the eighteenth century. The United States claimed Greenland for a short period of time in the early 1900s, and Dutch whalers and tradesmen have been in evidence from the beginning of the seventeenth century. The first Danish mission was established in 1721, which marks the beginning of the formal period of Danish colonialism. During World War II, the United States assumed protective custody of Greenland and established military bases on the island. Denmark was under German occupation at the time and supported the American action, which recognized Danish sovereignty over Greenland. One American military base remains at the town of Thule. Both American and Danish cultural influences can be found in contemporary Greenlandic society.

Elected municipal councils and two regional councils were established in 1910. In 1950, the two regional councils merged into a national council with the Danish governor sitting as chair. In 1953, Greenland became a country within Denmark, marking the end of the formal colonial period. In the post-1953 era, Danish administrators and teachers were attracted to Greenland through economic, housing and social benefits similar to those offered by the Canadian government in the Arctic (northern allowances, isolation pay, tax

Part I

benefits, housing, etc.). Some have argued that colonialism was actually intensified under these new arrangements: "Greenland was in fact more than ever governed politically, economically, intellectually, and physically by another people" (Petersen, 1995:5). This continued until the country achieved Home Rule in 1979, and perhaps beyond.

Writing about social change among Inuit in the circumpolar world, Bjerregaard and Young state: "In a given community, the initial phase of profound change can be said to begin with the first major epidemic and last until the whole community is Christianized" (1998:227). Prior to colonization, medical treatment in Greenland was provided by shamans or *angakkuq*. They mediated the spirit world and also performed surgery, such as operations for cataracts. Less often, treatment included the use of herbal remedies, such as Labrador tea and roseroot. In response to a health survey carried out in 1993 to 1994, only 45 out of 1,580 Greenlanders interviewed reported having used traditional treatments in the past two weeks (Bjerregaard and Young, 1998). The first district medical officers were appointed in 1839. Today, 16 of 18 districts (called municipalities) have a health post or small hospital. A central hospital is located in Nuuk and specialized services are treated in Denmark.

The history of education in Greenland is summarized in an article by Karl Kristian Olsen, director of Inerisaavik, an organization created under the 1990 *School Act* to oversee teaching methods and practice (Olsen, n.d.). Lutheran missionaries began teaching in schools soon after they first arrived in Greenland in 1721. In 1845, they set up a teachers' college to educate Greenlanders and, by the early 1900s, some students were being sent to Denmark for further education. Denmark legislated the first school act for Greenland in 1905. In 1928, Danish history and language were introduced into the curriculum. In the 1950s, the school system was separated from the church. Greenlandic became a subject in school, but the system itself continued to follow the Danish model (Petersen, 1995). In fact, the *Greenlandic School Act* of 1967 simply duplicated the Danish public school system and laws. Not until after Home Rule was established in 1979 did the language of instruction in schools change back to Greenlandic and the curriculum was shifted to include content more suitable to Greenlandic society. In the 1992-93 school year, there were almost twice as many Greenlandic than Danish teachers in the public school system, 498 Greenlanders compared to 270 Danish teachers, and all but 26 of 219 hourly instructors were Greenlandic (Olsen, n.d.). Ilisimatusarfik University, which offers courses at the bachelor and master levels for Greenlandic speaking students, was established in 1989.

Part I

Observations on Colonization in the United States, New Zealand, Australia and Greenland

Colonization proceeded along different paths in the United States, New Zealand, Australia and Greenland. In New Zealand, the *Treaty of Waitangi* defined the relationship between Maori and the Crown. The United States government negotiated treaties with some Aboriginal people prior to 1871, but, for the most part, efforts were concentrated on dispossessing Native Americans of their land. In both countries, treaty-making was followed by many years of warfare.

No treaties were signed in Australia. In fact, until 1992, the concept of Native title was totally denied by the national government. The political environment is one where, until very recently, Aboriginal people had few legal rights. Greenland is also without treaties, but because there is no private land ownership, the situation is very different. Also, Indigenous Greenlanders form the population majority and Greenlandic is the working language of government and business.

Differences also exist in the education system. Where the United States and Australia instituted a boarding school system similar to Canada's residential schools, New Zealand and Greenland had community schooling. In the United States, policy fluctuations resulted in periods where progressive attitudes prevailed in boarding schools toward Aboriginal culture; extra-curricular activities allowed Native American art, music, drama and dance to flourish. The situation was starkly different from that experienced by Aboriginal children in Australia where assimilationist policies were especially harsh.

The experiences of Indigenous people under colonialism also converge in a number of significant ways. Boarding schools in the United States and Australia shared a common goal of assimilating Aboriginal children into the dominant society and culture. Community schools in New Zealand had similar goals and Greenland inherited the Danish school system and curriculum. In all cases, colonialism seriously undermined Indigenous cultures, languages, lands and resources; political autonomy vanished. Depopulation resulted from the introduction of new diseases. In all four nation-states, Aboriginal people experience poorer health and lower social and economic status than non-Indigenous citizens. Part II of this report explores decolonization, a process that involves addressing historic trauma and unravelling the tragic aftereffects of colonization.

Part II

Decolonization and Healing

The previous section provided a brief overview of the colonization process in the United States, New Zealand, Australia and Greenland. In this section, the focus turns to healing. While colonization and decolonization are essentially sociopolitical processes,[17] individuals respond in very personal ways. Historic trauma theory (Wesley-Esquimaux and Smolewski, 2004; Duran and Duran, 1995) argues that individuals can be traumatized by events that occurred before their birth. "Hidden collective memories of this trauma, or a collective non-remembering, is passed from generation to generation, as are the maladaptive social and behavioural patterns that are symptoms of many social disorders caused by historic trauma" (Wesley-Esquimaux and Smolewski, 2004:iv). The roots of such trauma are found in the history of colonization:

> Indigenous social and cultural devastation in the present is the result of unremitting personal and collective trauma due to demographic collapse, resulting from early influenza and smallpox epidemics and other infectious diseases, conquest, warfare, slavery, colonization, proselytization, famine and starvation, the 1892 to the late 1960s residential school period and forced assimilation (Wesley-Esquimaux and Smolewski, 2004:1).

This does not mean that every Aboriginal person is being overwhelmed by historic trauma. Individuals and communities have vastly different experiences and histories, and the resulting trauma (or absence of trauma) will vary greatly. Healing and recovery are also influenced by a myriad of factors, including:

- individual experiences, strengths and resources;
- relationships within the family;
- community social, political and economic conditions;
- community culture, traditions, language, history, resources and governance;
- the degree of leadership support for healing; and
- community capacity, including access to experienced healers and therapists.

---

[17]   In his article, *Process of Decolonization*, Laenui states: "Colonization and decolonization are social processes even more than they are political processes. Governance over a people changes only after the people themselves have sufficiently changed" (2000:150). The term "sociopolitical" is used above to incorporate both elements and to ensure that the political dimensions are not lost.

Part II

In other words, a relationship exists between history, the social, economic and political environments and individual experiences. Therapeutic approaches to healing that incorporate Indigenous history will more effectively address root causes. At the same time, many individuals need therapeutic help to heal from deeply personal wounds or to address depression, addiction or the effects of physical and sexual abuse.

Table 2 juxtaposes the sociopolitical process of decolonization—the individual process of healing from post traumatic stress disorder (PTSD) and healing from historic trauma. Presented in this way, the similarities between these three processes are revealed. The first column presents Lanaui's process of decolonization, a corollary of the colonization process described in Part I. Decolonization proceeds through five stages: rediscovery and recovery of Indigenous history and culture; mourning; dreaming; commitment; and action (Laenui, 2000).

The second column sets out Judith Herman's stages of recovery from post traumatic stress disorder (PTSD). Herman has done groundbreaking work with individuals suffering from PTSD. She states that recovery unfolds in three stages: the first stage is the establishment of safety; the second stage is remembrance and mourning; and in the third stage, the individual reconnects with ordinary life (Herman, 1997).

The last column—healing from historic trauma—brings history and culture together with personal healing on a journey that is both individual and collective in nature; it is based on a combination of the first two columns. Lessons learned in research and evaluation studies undertaken for the Aboriginal Healing Foundation contributed to the development of this model (Kishk Anaquot Health Research, 2001; 2002; 2003; Wesley-Esquimaux and Smolewski, 2004). Healing from historic trauma begins with creating a personally and culturally safe environment where the impacts of history, including the legacy of abuse in residential and boarding schools, can be safely explored. Reconnecting with culture plays a significant role in this process. The second stage involves remembering and mourning personal losses, as well as those of parents, grandparents and ancestors. The final three stages are dreaming, building and rebuilding healthy relationships and giving back to family and community in the spirit of self-determination.

Table 2 is followed by examples of the decolonization process in each of the four nation-states under discussion. In the United States, the emergence of post-colonial psychology is discussed. This provides the theoretical basis for linking PTSD and historic trauma. A description of the revival of Maori culture and traditional healing within New Zealand society follows. Remembrance and mourning are discussed with a

Part II

focus on Australia; Aboriginal and Torres Strait Islander people have been struggling to come to terms with their colonial past and to have the injustice they suffered formally acknowledged by the national government. The final section looks at the success of Greenlanders in maintaining their language, but raises questions about the impact of colonization on Greenlandic culture and the health of the Greenlandic people.

These examples are representative of the earliest stages of decolonization and healing from historic trauma: cultural rediscovery; increased knowledge and understanding of Indigenous history and the impacts of colonization; and remembrance and mourning. Despite the usefulness of working with a model that depicts decolonization and healing as occurring in distinct stages, events do not naturally fit into neat categories, nor do they always occur in a linear way. Laenui acknowledges this and states that individuals and societies can revisit stages they passed through at an earlier time: "As one goes through the phases of rediscovery and recovery, then mourning, next dreaming, it is at times helpful or even necessary to return to rediscovery and recovery to aid in the dreaming" (2000:159).

Part II

Table 2) Decolonization and Healing

Laenui's Process of Decolonization	Judith Herman's Three Phases of Recovery from PTSD	Healing from Historic Trauma
Sociopolitical process	Personal journey	Personal and collective journey
Rediscovery and recovery: renewed interest in history, culture, music, art and literature, both traditional and modern; contributes to a recovery of pride	Safety: creating a safe environment, establishing trust in self and therapist	Personal and cultural safety: creating a safe environment; establishing trust; increasing knowledge and understanding of Indigenous and colonial history and its impacts; renewing interest in traditional culture, healing and spirituality
Mourning: an essential phase of decolonization is lamenting what was lost, a process that may include anger. Mourning can also accelerate the process of rediscovery and recovery, and the first two phases can feed each other	Remembrance and mourning: reconstructing and recounting the abuse story (events and feelings); integrating traumatic memories; mourning traumatic loss	Remembrance and mourning: speaking about and grieving personal losses and experiences of abuse, as well as those within the family and community/people (intergenerational impacts). Continued learning and building connections with culture, traditions, spirituality
Dreaming: fully exploring one's culture and traditions while building visions of the future		Dreaming: fully exploring one's culture and traditions while building a personal vision of the future
Commitment: making a personal commitment to working toward change	Reconnection: reconciling with oneself and relearning personal strengths; reconnecting with others	Connecting: affirming and rebuilding relationships within the family and community; developing new relationships
Action: the decolonization process culminates in proactive action in the spirit of self-determination		Giving back in the spirit of self-determination: contributing to family and community

Part II

United States: The Emergence of Post-Colonial Psychology

The United States literature on Aboriginal mental health and healing is strong in the realm of decolonization and post-colonial theory. The impacts of colonization, including the boarding school system, on Native American individuals, families and tribes are well recognized and documented. Eduardo Duran and Bonnie Duran (1995; 2000) are perhaps the best known proponents of post-colonial psychology and they developed a therapeutic treatment model that addresses the intergenerational effects of PTSD. The traditional component is critical to the model, including a Native American psychology and worldview rooted in the particular culture, values and tribal traditions of the client. Duran and Duran use the term "intergenerational post-traumatic stress disorder." They also state: "Many Native American people are diagnosed based on erroneous criteria; the diagnostic process never takes a historical perspective in the placing of a diagnosis on the client. The authors fantasize that one day the DSM-III [Diagnostic Statistical Manual for Mental Disorders] will have diagnostic criteria such as 'acute or chronic reaction to genocide and colonialism'" (2000:52-53).

The authors describe how this framework is put into practice. The program referred to is the San Francisco Bay Area Urban Model, developed by Eduardo Duran. This program has been deemed successful in that it serves hundreds of clients each month, many of whom have "returned for ongoing therapy twenty times, which is almost seven times the return rate in orthodox programs" (Duran and Duran, 1995:88) serving Native American clients. They report that, over time, the range of diagnostic categories was as varied as that of any group, although at least 75 per cent exhibited symptoms associated with PTSD. The therapeutic process includes culturally-based dream interpretation and Western psychotherapy. A therapeutic team composed of Western-trained counselors (psychologists), traditional counselors and medicine people are involved in the treatment process. Clients are referred to either the traditional counselor or psychologist who makes an initial assessment, but the course of treatment is developed by a team that includes all counselors, social workers and other providers in the agency. Normally, the treatment includes both psychotherapy and participation in traditional ceremonies; but, for many people, the most important step is to reconnect with their culture:

> Many Native American clients have been so acculturated that many times the focus of the therapy is merely to reconnect them to a traditional belief system and make sense of their lifeworld from a traditional perspective. Caution should be taken by the reader so that there will not be a confusion of traditional approaches and reconnection with the romanticizing of traditional that is so popular these days. The client must be helped to understand and to work

at coping in the actual lifeworld that is around them, and for the most part the client must be able to adjust and work in a white environment as well as still maintain a sense of identity. This is difficult if not impossible for the therapist who has not had to do so in his/her own life (Duran and Duran, 1995:89).

For the authors, reconnecting clients with their Native American identity improves self-esteem and sense of identity, which are correlated with healthy functioning. Further, an increased awareness of historical factors reduces guilt and internalized oppression. In Canada, evaluations of the Aboriginal Healing Foundation's program activity have led to similar conclusions. The first interim evaluation found that some of the most successful approaches to healing included traditional therapies and combining alternative and traditional therapies.

> Projects were also thrilled with their reinforcement of culture (43%) through the use of healing circles and ceremonies (e.g. sweat lodges, smudging). They were certain that using the language, sharing traditions, involving Elders, story telling and retreating to traditional camps facilitated the healing process (Kishk Anaquot Health Research, 2001:75).

The second interim evaluation reports that gaining a personal understanding of the legacy of physical and sexual abuse in residential schools can be a pivotal first step toward healing. "When history is shared, a social context is created for what is often viewed as an individual's problems" (Kishk Anaquot Health Research, 2002:30).

Duran and Duran contend that the effects of colonization are especially severe for men who, as warriors, were supposed to repel the oppressors and protect their families and communities. Coupled with the destruction of traditional economic and cultural roles, colonization has led to a "deep psychological trauma of identity loss" (Duran and Duran, 1995:36). A treatment model that addresses these issues is said to be effective in treating addictions and in addressing family violence: "There is no way that the client can begin to deal with the issues of violence in the family without understanding the dynamics of the historical violence perpetrated on Native American people by the European colonization process" (Duran and Duran, 1995:90).

Part II

New Zealand: Rediscovery and Recovery of Maori Culture

By the 1980s, a cultural renaissance was underway among Maori. Witi Ihimaera (1998) writes about the years of Maori protest from 1970 to 1990 that led to a resurgence of pride and a reclamation of identity. "From 1976, courses in Māori language were included in the curriculum of 5 universities and 8 training school colleges. In 1981 the first "kohanga reo" (language nest) pre-school Māori language immersion programme was established, led by Māori women. The aim was to make every Māori child bilingual by the age of 5 years old" (Whitmore, n.d.). In 1987, Maori was declared an official language of New Zealand. Maori language and culture are promoted under the *Broadcasting Act, 1989*, leading to the establishment of Maori radio and television stations. By 1994, there were 809 *kohanga reo* schools (Whitmore, n.d.). Still, the 1996 Census reported that only a quarter of adult men and women were able to speak Maori, the most fluent being over 65 years and the least fluent in the age group 20 to 39 years (Statistics New Zealand, 1998).

The cultural renaissance resulted in a greater awareness of colonialism and its impacts. This led to an increased focus on the *Treaty of Waitangi* as the basis of Maori relationships with the Crown. Settlements of claims based on the treaty have been under negotiation, and the financial part of settlements has allowed some tribes to establish social and mental health services. The treaty is interpreted as protecting Maori intellectual property, recognizing Maori perspectives of health, and giving Maori the right to engage in their cultural traditions, including traditional healing (Jones, 2000b).

In 1993, the National Body of Traditional Maori Healers was established and, today, traditional healing is offered in many primary health care settings. This body recognizes regional and tribal variations in healing traditions, but it also works to achieve a collective approach to issues, such as professional standards, policy and access to funding. Traditional healers offer a variety of treatments, including herbal medicine, physiotherapy and spiritual healing. The Ministry of Health has published standards for traditional Maori healing, developed with the support from the National Body of Traditional Maori Healers. Included in the publication are standards of practice, referrals, record keeping, patient rights and responsibilities, training, liaison and networking, protection of *rongoa* (traditional medicine produced from native plants), collection, preparation, storage and labelling of *rongoa*, and prescription and dispensing standards (New Zealand Ministry of Health, 1999). Government reforms in the 1980s and 1990s led to increased privatization of health services, which has actually provided opportunities for Maori *whanau, hapu, iwi* and community groups to take over the delivery of programs and services and become a "provider" (Pipi et. al., 2002). The Ministry of Health defines a Maori health provider as *"an independent Maori health provider whose services are targeted towards Maori, and have a Maori management and governance structure"* (New Zealand Ministry of Health, 2002:2).

The way the New Zealand government has embraced Maori culture without necessarily supporting the empowerment of Maori has not been without criticism. For example, Juan Marrcellus Tauri (1998) argued that *indigenization*[18] has permeated government policy, legislation and service delivery. Examples include the appointment of a Maori Elder as institutional patron and government departments adopting Maori names, songs and motifs. Family group conferencing, in particular, is seen as representing an indigenization of New Zealand's justice system, rather than empowerment of Maori. Beginning in 1989, the justice system formally incorporated family group conferencing as one means of addressing youth in conflict with the law. Family group conferences involve the young people who committed the crime and their families; the victims (or their representatives), their families and other supports; police; and, sometimes, social workers and lawyers. Tauri contends that the process is actually disempowering, for it employs the state's justice processes while denying Maori a significant measure of jurisdictional autonomy.

In light of such criticism, it could be argued that the government's role in the Maori renaissance is reflective of the transformation/exploitation stage of colonization as defined by Laenui (2000). On the other hand, the vitality of the literature, much of it written by Maori people, is more in line with the first stage of decolonization—rediscovery and recovery. The *Treaty of Waitangi* has a prominent place in both Maori writing and government publications. The treaty's importance extends far beyond the symbolic—it has both legal and political significance. While the impacts of colonialism continue to be evidenced in socioeconomic statistics, it is clear that Maori are working effectively to transform, not only these statistics, but also the social and political environments of New Zealand/Aotearoa.

Australia: Struggling to Come to Terms with Historic Injustice

In 1991, the Royal Commission into Aboriginal Deaths in Custody issued an 11-volume report on the results of its wide-ranging inquiry into Aboriginal people and the criminal justice system. Among the findings is

---

[18]   Indigenization is defined as the involvement of Indigenous people and organizations in the delivery of existing socio-legal services and programs. This definition is attributed to Finkler (1990) who includes programs to recruit First Nations courtworkers, police officers and prison personnel as part of Canada's indigenization program, along with sentencing circles and alternatives to incarceration for Aboriginal offenders.

Part II

evidence of overrepresentation of Aboriginal people in the criminal justice system. In Western Australia, Aboriginal people were 43 times as likely to be in police custody and 26 times more likely to be in prison (Fryer-Smith, 2002). Investigations of 99 people who died in prison found that 43 had been removed from their families by the state: "The Royal Commissioner concluded that the enduring legacy of British colonisation and post-colonial laws and practices was systemic Aboriginal socio-economic disadvantage, disempowerment and cultural fragmentation" (Fryer-Smith, 2002:1:6).

The 1997 report of the Human Rights and Equal Opportunity Commission, *Bringing Them Home*, opened the door to redressing this enduring legacy of British colonialism with respect to the generations of children who were placed in institutions and foster homes. Reconciliation Australia, a non-profit organization established in December 2000, speaks about the difficulties in moving forward, of healing without a "frank and honest acknowledgment" that government policies were wrong and harmful. The organization's role is to report on progress, circulate information, encourage partnerships and provide forums for discussion on the reconciliation process (Reconciliation Australia, 2002). Report cards are issued that monitor and assess progress against benchmarks based on the recommendations made by its predecessor, the Council for Aboriginal Reconciliation.[19] The 2002 Report Card, *Words, Symbols and Actions*, refers to the memory of reconciliation walks in 2000 that saw the involvement of over one million people, but notes that tangible outcomes in policy and practice are also required.

Overall, the national government's response to the recommendations of the Council for Aboriginal Reconciliation was considered inadequate. While the need for improved outcomes in health, education and standard of living was recognized, it either ignored or rejected recognition "of the rights of Aboriginal and Torres Strait Islander peoples that are theirs and theirs alone as the first peoples of this country" (Reconciliation Australia 2002:7). These rights include customary law and self-determination. Concerns were also raised regarding the government's continued failure to apologize and its rejection of a process to negotiate a treaty to protect political, legal, cultural and economic rights. The failure to pursue a preamble to the Constitution recognizing Aboriginal and Torres Strait Islander people as First Peoples was also noted.

The process of reconciliation bogs down in what should logically be the first step: an apology. The commonwealth government has issued a statement of regret, but it was "rejected by many Indigenous and

---

[19] Recommendations are contained in the report, *Reconciliation: Australia's Challenge*, released in December 2000.

other Australians as inadequate. The government's reluctance to offer an apology still casts a shadow over the reconciliation process, sending mixed signals to both Indigenous people and the wider community" (Reconciliation Australia, 2002:26). Some movement, however, is being made on other fronts. Beginning in 1998, May 26 became acknowledged as *Sorry Day*. More than one million people have signed *Sorry Books*. By 2002, all state and territory parliaments and the Commonwealth senate had apologized, as well as many local councils. However, as noted, the federal government only issued a statement of regret.

At a national Stolen Generations Conference in 2001, Race Discrimination Commissioner Dr. William Jonas referred to the progress being made in Canada—the Law Commission of Canada's report on institutional child abuse, the federal government's 1998 *Statement of Reconciliation* and the creation of the Aboriginal Healing Foundation. Lamenting the lack of progress in Australia, he suggests the country was out of step with international trends: "The refusal to apologize formally to members of the stolen generation for past injustices, the failure to develop comprehensive reparation programs, and the promotion of litigation as an appropriate redress mechanism are contrary to a world-wide trend" (Jonas, 2001:13). In another presentation, Shelly Reys, co-chair of Reconciliation Australia, argued passionately that all Australians need to admit the events documented in the *Bringing Them Home* report took place. Such arguments are deemed necessary in light of comments by federal government ministers who imply that children may not have been "stolen" as much as "removed" from undesirable situations. She fears that, for some people, the word "stolen" only applied to those children who were snatched from their mothers' arms kicking and screaming.

In the absence of a formal apology and support for healing through funded programs, it is not surprising that Australia looks to Canada as a model. Public debate in Australia remains focused on the issue of recognizing historical injustices and the resulting trauma. Professor Lowitja O'Donoghue (2001), another speaker at the Stolen Generations Conference and a member of the stolen generations, spoke about her personal priorities: access to personal and family records (many still do not know who their families are and, therefore, have not reestablished contact); family tracing and reunion services; appropriate Indigenous health services to heal loss and grief and training for health care workers; and reforms to the child welfare and juvenile justice system to ensure there are guarantees against repetition.

In spite of the volumes of official documents on the forced removal of Indigenous children and the trauma and social disintegration that followed, denial continues to operate as an obstacle to reconciliation and healing. This has implications for the design and delivery of therapeutic healing services. A paper on the therapeutic needs of Indigenous male offenders mentions a variety of treatments that could work, but stipulates they must also address historical issues, such as the impact of colonization:

> To think that a short cognitive-behavioural based treatment programme will in some way address the Aboriginal client's treatment issues is naïve, when consideration is given to what an individual will bring with them to the treatment forum. And to think that these unique Aboriginal ways of being can be modularized within a cognitive-behavioural program is also naïve. These historical issues, are very complex and require a cultural healing paradigm to address them (Yavu-Kama-Harathunian, 2002:17).

Yavu-Kama-Harathunian also stresses the need to involve the client's family and community, for the treatment process to include spiritual healing and ceremonies within a cultural healing model and, especially, to have the program design rest with Aboriginal people.

Greenland: Geographic Isolation as Protection?

The colonization process in Greenland appears to have been less overtly brutal than in the United States, Australia and New Zealand. Protective factors likely include the island's geographical isolation and Arctic climate and environment. Inuit constitute about 80 per cent of the population, compared to 15 per cent in New Zealand and less than 3 per cent in Australia and the United States. Greenlandic is an official working language in schools, government and business. While Denmark's colonizing influence is certainly felt, the fact that Inuit have remained the majority population had a mitigating effect.

Yet, social problems certainly exist. For example, 25 per cent of women and 6 per cent of men who responded to Greenland's 1993-94 Health Interview Survey reported having been sexually abused at some point in their lives. For those women who reported the identity of the offender, 30 per cent identified a family member, 18 per cent identified an acquaintance, and 43 per cent reported a person more distant than a family member or an acquaintance. Twenty-one per cent of the men identified the offender as a family member (Curtis et. al., 2002). Bjerregaard and Young report that homicide rates have increased greatly since 1940: "Much violence in Greenland is performed by young men who, under the influence of alcohol, attack their spouse, who is often also intoxicated" (1998:145).

Part II

A study comparing suicide rates in Greenland, Alaska and the Northwest Territories during the period 1968 to 1996 found that Greenland had the highest overall suicide rate; and persons born in Greenland had the highest rate of all (Jensen, 1999). The study found a positive correlation between suicide rates and alcohol consumption, but no relationship between unemployment and suicide. Within Greenland, rates were highest in the northeast region, a part of the country that was colonialized relatively late. The study concludes that people born in the Northeast have had a shorter period of time to adjust to colonial rule and are, therefore, experiencing a higher degree of assimilation accompanied by higher levels of stress. Despite having achieved home rule, Jensen reports that many Greenlanders continue to view the government as colonial because the administrative system duplicates the Danish system. A more recent study confirms the findings of high suicide rates among Inuit in Greenland, but reports they appear to have stabilized between 1990 and 1995 (Leineweber and Arensman, 2003).

Bjerregaard and Young (1998) refer to controversial interpretations of studies[20] that report the highest suicide rates in less developed towns, and among hunters, fishermen and unemployed people within the towns. The findings are interpreted as being the result of social changes not happening fast enough to meet expectations. Bjerregaard and Young (1998), on the other hand, cite an epidemiological study that finds a positive correlation at the community level between population increase and suicides and, in West Greenland, between community size and suicides (i.e., the highest suicide rates were in large and growing communities). "After controlling for age and sex, suicidal thoughts are found to be more prevalent in residents of Nuuk and towns on the east coast than in the rest of the country, and more prevalent in those with the least traditional childhood and who speak the least Greenlandic" (Bjerregaard and Young, 1998:155). In other words, a more traditional lifestyle mitigates against suicide.

High suicide rates also plague Inuit in Canada who, like Greenlanders, have retained their language and have maintained a connection with their culture. However, traditional lifestyles and economies in Greenland and the Canadian Arctic have undergone profound changes during the past century. With respect to Inuit throughout the circumpolar world:

---

[20]   The authors refer to suicide studies by Jørgen Thorslund and J.C. Misfeldt (1989). On suicide statistics. Arctic Medical Research 48(3):124-130; (1990) Inuit suicides in Greenland. Arctic Medical Research 49(1):25-33; and (1992) Ungdomsselvmord og moderniserings probemer blandt Inuit i Grøland. Holte: SOCPOL.

Part II

The influx of non-Inuit people, rapid growth of the Inuit population, and increasing concentration in larger communities of up to several thousand inhabitants have profoundly altered the social structure of Inuit communities. Together with other sociocultural changes, this has resulted in acculturative stress and increased prevalence of mental health problems including suicides (Bjerregaard and Young, 1998:231).

In summary, Greenlandic Inuit, despite the benefits of being a population majority and having achieved a level of political self-determination, have distressingly high suicide rates. While a variety of explanations have been put forward to account for high suicide rates, no broad consensus on solutions has been achieved. Social problems in Greenland, like those that beset Indigenous people in colonized nations elsewhere, may, over time, respond to the positive influences of decolonization. Certainly, the legacy of colonization cannot be discounted.

Part III

Promising Healing Practices

In this report, promising healing practices refer to models, approaches, techniques and initiatives that are based on Indigenous experience and that result in positive changes in people's lives. All of the examples have roots in Indigenous traditions, values and culture. Many also include Western or mainstream practices. The examples provided below are drawn from the literature reviewed for this report and the same limitations apply. Greenland, in particular, is not well represented due to the lack of published information in English. While there were no formal selection criteria, the principles outlined below were used as a general guideline.

The Assembly of First Nations (1997a) identified the following common strengths among the projects it reviewed in a paper on successful Indigenous health programs in Canada, the United States and Australia:

- projects tend to be tradition-based and values-based;
- interventions focus on the entire family;
- links are made between spirituality and therapy;
- there is an intimate knowledge of the tribal community and a drawing together of traditions;
- projects respond to the needs of the community; and
- the community supported healing and recovery.

Success is based on a variety of factors: the skills of the community; use of local staff; extended hours of service; integrated services; and holistic strategies. These strengths are evident in many of the programs outlined below.

Tohunga: **Traditional Maori Healers (New Zealand):** In 2000, Rhys Jones published a qualitative study describing an urban *rongoa* Maori clinic in Auckland that employs traditional healers or *tohunga*. During in-depth interviews with four of the healers, he found that three had some Western training (two in nursing and one in massage) and that traditional healing was learned through a variety of informal routes: observing an experienced healer, self-study, learning from mistakes, asking questions and "prayer and dedication." One healer had spent many years collecting and preparing *rongoa*. The two principal healers at the centre, one of whom had twenty years experience, are considered the main source of knowledge by the others. "A common theme that emerged during interviews with the participants was a family history of traditional healing although, in general, most of their personal knowledge had come from non family sources" (Jones, 2000a:19).

Part III

The healers described the framework they work with as the five cornerstones of healing—spiritual, mental, physical, family and education—all five are considered necessary. The healing process uses the strongest dimension to help the others: "A lot of ostensibly physical problems were in fact believed to be caused by spiritual, psychological and family issues" (Jones, 2000a:19). Many patients who used the clinic had already consulted a doctor and had a diagnosis, which the healer would attempt to confirm as well as understand the underlying cause. Diagnosis consisted of gathering a detailed patient history, including information about the present problem, symptoms, previous illnesses, medications, occupation, social considerations and family history. This would be followed by a physical examination. "Two of the healers used a special ability to see inside the patient's body, which could be likened to performing a scan. By knowing what each part of the body normally looked like, it was possible to identify any abnormalities" (Jones, 2000a:21). One mentioned being able to see blockages, infections and "missing pieces," such as a gallbladder that had been removed. Another could feel heat as she passed her hands over an affected area.

Jones notes similarities between traditional and Western diagnosis, including a step-by-step investigative diagnostic process and referral for a second opinion. A major difference relates to the almost exclusive focus on the physical in Western medicine, along with greater specificity and more emphasis on the diagnostic label. Traditional healers place a greater emphasis on the spiritual dimension.

In a separate article on traditional Maori healing, Jones raises questions about how to protect *rongoa* Maori (traditional medicine) from exploitation: "Essentially, there exists a tension between protecting rongoa Maori as a taonga [treasure] and utilising it for health gains" (Jones, 2000c:107). Since many people consult both traditional and Western practitioners about the same problem, the potential exists for conflicting advice and negative pharmacological interactions. He concludes that the two can coexist, with the most exciting partnership potential being among Maori health providers and traditional healers at the local or *iwi* level.

Dedicated Maori Alcohol and Drug Treatment (New Zealand): In the alcohol and drug treatment field, a number of Maori-specific treatment units have been established. Evaluations of these services have examined participation and patient satisfaction, as well as the characteristics of individuals participating in dedicated Maori and mainstream services (Huriwai et. al., 1998; 2000; 2001). There are links between cultural esteem and mental health and the likelihood that a positive cultural identity protects against poor health. While evaluations have not addressed the effectiveness of culturally-based treatment, they suggest that access to services is improved by the provision of dedicated Maori services. In addition, clients of dedicated Maori services were five and a half times more likely to be satisfied with treatment (Huriwai et. al., 2000).

The research on Maori-dedicated treatment programs casts a light on the difficulties surrounding culture-based treatment for Maori who are not well connected to their traditional family, *iwi* and culture. Concerns have been raised that treatment based on generic views of Maori culture fails to recognize that cultural knowledge and traditions were traditionally localized in the extended family, sub-tribe and tribe. Similar challenges are faced in North American cities where Aboriginal people seeking healing come from a variety of cultures and nations. Huriwai and his colleagues stressed moving beyond a "stereotypical and sometimes romantic view of Māori and *whānau* assumes that all Māori have the same attitudes, behaviours and values" (2001:1043). Further research has been suggested in the development of culturally-sensitive instruments to measure changes in connectedness to family, culture and traditions. "An implication of this is that Māori, regardless of their apparent level of acculturation, may benefit from processes and practices that would increase "cultural connectedness." " (Huriwai et. al., 2000:291).

Ti Piriti Treatment Program for Sexual Offenders (New Zealand): The role of culture was also central to an examination of a voluntary treatment program in Auckland for incarcerated Maori men who have sexually offended against children.[21] The program uses cognitive, behavioural and social learning concepts woven with cultural values and activities. The program is "embedded in a Western psychological context, but extensive efforts have been made to maximize the impact of input from Māori" (Robertson et. al., 1999:199). The Ti Piriti mission statement acknowledges Maori beliefs, values and rights by referencing the *Treaty of Waitangi*. The statement also expresses the program's commitment to biculturalism, such as ethnically diverse staff, a culturally supportive environment and development of processes for connecting with local *iwi* and other Maori. In contrast to the dedicated Maori alcohol and drug treatment program discussed above, this one is purposefully bicultural in nature. A cultural consultant conducts cultural assessments aimed at uncovering the effects of colonization on the client and the extent of their knowledge of, and comfort with, Maori and *Pakeha* (non-Maori) cultures. The assessment process can lead to recommendations for English or Maori language classes and referrals to Maori healers and teachers (Larsen et. al., 1998). Other cultural components include a weekly Maori caucus with instruction in Maori beliefs, values and practices and integrating

---

[21]   The overall program sounds similar to the Waseya Holistic Treatment Program for Aboriginal offenders offered at Waseskun Healing Lodge in Quebec and funded by the Aboriginal Healing Foundation.

traditional welcoming ceremonies into the program. "Incorporation of central aspects of Maori society in the program helps to reverse the negative impact of colonization by validating traditional beliefs and attitudes, thus facilitating acculturation into Maori society in parallel with increasing acculturation into Pakeha society" (Larsen et. al., 1998:391). The authors report an increase in both the number of Maori in treatment as well as in the number who complete the program.

Nonverbal Therapies (Australia): Working with Aboriginal prisoners in Australia, Yava-Kamu-Harathunian found that psychodrama and art therapy respond to spiritual treatment needs. "Through art, dance, drama, music, song and chant/mantra meditation techniques which include practiced silence, the practitioner can guide a client to experience both positive and not positive feelings, situations, options, thought systems, and assist the client to build upon their personal commitment to experience flexibility, change and wellness" (Yava-Kamu-Harathunian, 2002:13).

Narrative Therapy (Australia): A paper prepared for the Assembly of First Nations (1997b) profiles a narrative therapy project that took place in Australia at a weeklong healing camp. Narrative therapy was developed by two non-Aboriginal family therapists, Michael White and David Epston,[22] who believe it is possible to work with individual, family and cultural stories and experiences. The approach has been adapted by some Aboriginal organizations that see its potential as a process that allows grief to be expressed publicly. People are able to confront problems in their lives through learning to tell a different story and developing a new understanding of the reality of their lives and relationships. Missing information, including historical information about government policies impacting on Indigenous people, cultural values and perspectives, and traditional strengths and skills, can be incorporated into the new story. This reduces guilt and places the blame for social and economic problems outside of the individual. At the same time, narrative therapy creates an awareness of the wider political, racial, gender and cultural contexts.

Navajo Peacekeeping (United States): The traditional Navajo practice of peacekeeping has been used effectively as a response to family violence. Robert Yazzie (2000) describes how Navajo women are offered a choice between Western restraining orders and traditional Navajo peacemaking in cases of domestic violence. If peacekeeping is chosen, the following process is used:

---

[22]   The Dulwich Centre (www.dulwichcentre.com.au) is considered the home of narrative therapy. Narrative therapy appears to be growing in popularity far beyond Australia; for example, an international conference was held at Spelman College in the United States in June 2002 where Cherokee Nations came together with African Americans, Aboriginal Australians, Latinos, Maoris, Swedes, Canadians, Samoans, Norwegians and many others.

Part III

The session opens with a prayer said by the peacemaker or a respected family member. Prayer is important because peacemaking is actually a healing ceremony, and prayer gets people to commit to the peacemaking process. Next, the people who are gathered start to "talking out" their problem. The woman gets to do something she cannot do in a courtroom: she vents her emotions and tells the group how she feels about the event. ... The man then describes his feelings (Yazzie, 2000:44-45).

Many men give excuses, such as "she asked for it" or he had too much to drink, and this process is important in determining what motivated him to commit the offence. The peacemaker or, sometimes, other participants can then deal with such false excuses. Peacemakers are not expected to be neutral mediators—they are chosen because of their respected position in the community as "planners and teachers who have definite opinions when something goes wrong" (Yazzie, 2000:44-45). When it is time to discuss solutions, all participants are brought into the planning process. The plan can include addressing an underlying alcohol or drug problem, a program of spirituality and ceremonies "to correct false assumptions and attitudes" or participation in Western violence-control counseling. Moreover, the process is not based on the assumption that the couple should stay together: "The peacemaking can conclude with a reconciliation between the man and woman or a family discussion and consensus about ending the marriage for the good of the parties and their families" (Yazzie, 2000:45).

The utilization of traditional peacekeeping is part of a process of arriving at "an internal sovereignty," of declaring community and spiritual independence in the face of the myriad of problems and issues that no one at the community level can control:

The best response to violence is healing. ...While Indigenous peoples may not succeed with "macro" issues such as jurisdiction, land-use control, or dealing with outsiders and intruders, they can succeed with "micro" issues. Taking control of one's own life is a healing issue. Strengthening the family is healing. Communities must consider how they can effectively reassume control of their destinies (Yazzie, 2000:47).

Reasons for Living Inventory (United States): The Reasons for Living (RFL) inventory is a "strengths-based" screening tool used for assessing suicide risk. Various versions of the tool have been tested cross-culturally, although no evaluation has examined its clinical usefulness, validity and reliability with American Indian adolescents (Graham, 2002). Thomas Crofoot Graham of Portland State University argues that the RFL inventory can be used effectively with Aboriginal youth to identify potential areas of intervention: "Using these assessment tools, a practitioner could help American Indian adolescents assess where they may be out of balance and help them connect with traditional healing approaches to further support their growth" (Graham, 2002:71). RFL inventories can be used to draw out spiritual beliefs, to identify supportive friends and family members and, within talking circles, to help youth identify their personal reasons for living. Questions cover spiritual issues (moral objections, religious beliefs); mind (future optimism, suicide-related concerns, self-acceptance, survival and coping beliefs); body (hurt, suffering, pain); and context (family and peer acceptance, social disapproval). However, while the overall subject areas complement a holistic and relational worldview, the content needs to be more culturally relevant. Graham recommends including questions about spiritual connections, participation in ceremonies and connection to nature, culture and community. Graham notes the need for a RFL assessment tool designed specifically for American Indian youth to be used by practitioners who have an understanding of Native American history and the impacts of colonization and who can connect youth to Indigenous healing traditions.

Youth at Risk Screening Tool (Australia): Dr. Tracey Westerman, the first Aboriginal woman in Australia to receive a Ph.D. in clinical psychology, developed a culturally-appropriate screening tool to help identify people at the early stages of crisis. The development process included focus groups of youth, parents and youth workers. The Westerman Aboriginal Symptom Checklist for Youth (WASC-Y) is now being used in schools to identify children at risk, who are then referred for treatment. The combined use of screening tools, culturally appropriate treatment and training for youth and adults has affected the suicide rate in Western Australia, which has dropped from one per month to only one death by suicide since July 2002 (Henderson, 2003).

Traditional Camp for Youth (United States): *Encouraging Leaders Dedicated to Enriching Respect and Spirituality* (E.L.D.E.R.S.) is an annual one-week camping event in New York State (Skye, 2002). This event focuses on providing youth with a holistic cultural experience. Organizers believe the experience promotes the development of a healthy self-identity and, also, that a lack of exposure to traditional beliefs and values contributes to increased levels of substance abuse.

Part III

At the camp, youth learn from Haudenosaunee Elders and their culturally-aware peers. Activities include learning the traditional Thanksgiving address, ceremonial dances (including the provision of information on the importance and meaning of the dances), traditional games (such as lacrosse), beading, basket weaving, talking circles, preparing traditional foods (corn, beans and squash, the "Three Sisters") and teachings based on wampum belts and the role of treaties. Some language instruction takes place, along with support for continued learning when they return to their community. Elders use the Seneca language, while some attendees speak Mohawk.

One theme of the camp is being of service to the community—in the camp environment, this involves preparing meals:

> Many of the traditional dishes, such as corn soup, require diligence, time, and much work in order for it to be prepared successfully. Being of service to the community in preparing the food is as much a symbolic need as it is one of necessity. Service to the community is seen as vital to the success of this and other such camping experiences. A Cherokee youth fitness camp reports similar success when promoting cultural retention through practicing of traditional values, beliefs, and approaches to spirituality, particularly when focusing on the importance of service to the community (Skye, 2002:130).

School of Life (Greenland): Knud Rasmussen College is a noncertificate school that began in the 1960s as a folk high school for Kalaallisut-speaking students. Students study Kalaallisut, history, social sciences, literature, math, Danish and English, as well as tanning, handicrafts, beadwork, stone polishing, science, geography, singing and computer sciences. In the spring, they work on the land to harvest food.

Cultural Safety (New Zealand): In New Zealand, teaching cultural safety has been incorporated into nursing and midwifery training courses since 1992 (Ellison-Loschmann and Pearce, 2000). Cultural safety includes providing services in an environment consistent with, and responsive to, Maori values, beliefs and practices, while challenging racial stereotypes. Cultural safety has also been woven into definitions of *kaupapa* Maori research (Cunningham, 2000).

Part III

O'odham Himdag as a Source of Strength and Wellness (United States): The Tohono O'odham in southern Arizona and northern Mexico, with 24,000 enrolled members and the second largest reservation in the American Southwest, have used 70 million dollars in annual revenues from two casinos to create jobs and develop a range of language, health and social programs. Services include a nursing home and a community college. All programs and services consciously maintain tribal traditions and cultural identity, and they are staffed and administered by O'odham people. The community has a high level of self-determination (Woods et. al., 2002).

O'odham Himdag (the O'odham path or way of life) includes language, which had been prohibited in the early mission school days and, later, when children were sent away to boarding schools. Today, the Tohono O'odham language is taught on the reservation at the San Xavier Mission School and the principal reports learning the language has done wonders for the children's self-esteem. Incorporated into a group therapy program for court-mandated youth, the Tohono O'odham language "provides culturally relevant words for feeling states that do not necessarily have an equivalent in English" (Woods et. al., 2002:42).

Port Augusta Families Project (South Australia): The Families Project in Port Augusta is a service for Aboriginal people and families who have multiple problems, many of which can be traced back to forced separation of family members. Project outcomes include breaking the cross-generational cycle that began with these disruptions. Families are given the opportunity to identify their own goals and staff work on the principles of empowerment, partnership and collaboration to ensure the process is in line with the family's wishes. Success stories include preventing the need for children to be placed in alternative care, repayment of debts, the return of children to the education system, stability in accommodation for the family and discharging of criminal justice orders. An Elders' group provides guidance and support to the project. While no details were provided on the treatment method, it appears to be based on a combination of practical interventions, support and empowerment (Kotz, 2001).

Integrated Health Services (Australia): Nunkuwarrin Yunti, a community centre in South Australia, has a health service that provides a wide variety of interventions: clinical services; a holistic model of healing that incorporates massage, Reiki and other alternative approaches; alcohol and drug treatment; youth-based service; a gym; and a place for community gatherings and meetings. The centre also provides narrative therapy and is developing curricula on Aboriginal mental health issues in partnership with universities. The importance of developing region- or group-specific healing models was stressed, along with different models for urban, rural and remote areas (Parliament of Australia, 1998).

Ali Curang Law and Justice Project (Australia): This project has been named a best practice model for addressing law and justice issues, especially with respect to family violence. Developed through a community consultation process, the model is based on Aboriginal dispute resolution, customary problem-solving techniques and the involvement of community organizations, Elders and traditional owners. The model is considered "an innovative adaptation of culturally relevant decision making, merged with mainstream law and justice" (Brown and Hayes, 2002:4).

Ali-Curung is a community with a population of about 500 established in the 1950s under government relocation policies. This is not a homogeneous community as there are four main language groups, and each group has different obligations related to family, land and ceremony. Relationships between the groups are not always friendly. Traditional land-owning groups have concerns about the influence of nontraditional groups in community affairs. For example, the Aboriginal community police officer was not from the area and, therefore, from a traditional perspective, should not have been involved in justice issues on land not his own. Some men did not support the development of a safe house, arguing that its proposed location was too near an area known to be inhabited by dangerous spirits. Over time, strategies were developed to address these issues (Brown and Hayes, 2002).

Aboriginal community safe houses function in conjunction with all other community organizations, groups, structures and decision-making processes. The project used paintings by community members that show the safe house, the cycle of violence and its impact on family members. Some of the paintings depict children, clients and staff at the safe house while the husband is drinking with the men. These have been used within the community to bring shame to men who neglect their duties as father and as husband. *"The use of shame has long been a powerful ingredient for social control among aboriginal people and this painting is used effectively by the women in community forums for that purpose"* (Brown and Hayes, 2002:9).

Kaupapa Maori Research (New Zealand): The resurgence of Maori culture has significantly changed the political landscape of New Zealand. This has not only influenced the delivery of health, social and educational programs, but has also influenced the research field. *Kaupapa* Maori research challenges Western assumptions about the generation of knowledge, stressing principles, such as Maori control, and the need for research to make a positive difference in Maori lives (Barnes, 2000; Cunningham, 2000; Smith, 1999). Language is important to research since Maori worldviews are embedded in language (Smith, 1999). "The language, in this sense, is a window to ways of knowing the world" (Smith, 1999:9) that would be otherwise unavailable. The potential of *kaupapa* Maori research is quite dramatic:

> The existence of a specific Māori epistemological base, redress of lost knowledge and protection of taonga under the Treaty of Waitangi, the usefulness of Māori knowledge and Māori analysis for Māori development, capitalising on the existing investment and promise of Māori medium education and the increasing importance of an [sic] global knowledge-base are each sound reasons for supporting the growth and development of kaupapa Māori research (Cunningham, 2000:68).

The growing body of published reports by Maori researchers, both descriptive and evaluative, provides a means of documenting and disseminating information about programs and services that are working well.

Principles of Good Practice: National Health and Medical Research Council (Australia): While recognizing that over two hundred years of colonization is the single most important factor contributing to the poor health status of Aboriginal and Torres Strait Islanders, Australia's National Health and Medical Research Council (NHMRC) wanted to recognize the positive work being undertaken by many communities. Nine projects were chosen to represent a variety of regions and health issues. These are outlined in a publication as case studies, along with the following set of principles of good practice (Australia NHMRC, 1996):

- needs identified by the community;
- partnerships between Indigenous health workers, communities and non-Indigenous health workers;
- resources and organizational support;
- implementation in the control of communities and Indigenous health workers;
- outcomes identified; and
- sustainability.

Conclusions

Learning Across Cultures and Nations

Indigenous people in the United States, New Zealand, Australia and Greenland share with Aboriginal people in Canada the experience of being colonized. The devastating impact of the past on the present becomes apparent when history and the experience of being colonized are woven into a search for approaches to healing that work well for Indigenous people. Similarities and differences in history and context can be observed across nation-states and, in the process, patterns sometime emerge. With respect to Indigenous people in the United States, New Zealand, Australia and Greenland, clear and distinct patterns are seen.

The experience of being colonized involves loss—of culture, language, land, resources, political autonomy, religious freedom and, often, personal autonomy. These losses may have a direct relationship to the poor health, social and economic status of Indigenous people. Understanding the need for personal and collective healing from this perspective points to a way of healing, one that combines the sociopolitical work involved in decolonization with the more personal therapeutic healing journey.

Groundbreaking research and theoretical work on treating the effects of intergenerational and historic trauma have emerged during the past decade. Such research opens the door to new approaches to healing that are especially relevant to working with Survivors of residential and boarding schools. Learning about the history of colonization, mourning the losses and reconnecting with traditional cultures, values and practices are becoming recognized stages of the healing process. Indigenous people in the United States, Australia and New Zealand, as well as Canada, are all addressing historic trauma, both at a theoretical level and within therapeutic practice. This supports an early finding of the Aboriginal Healing Foundation: education about residential schools is not only an effective way to dismantle denial, but it also acts as a catalyst for individuals to engage in healing.

Cultural intervention plays a vital role in the health and healing fields. Solid arguments can be made in favour of embedding healing practices in the specific cultures, traditions and languages of Indigenous people, nations, tribes and communities. At the same time, pan-Aboriginal approaches and the sharing of Indigenous healing traditions across cultures are a growing phenomena. Even ceremonies, which tend to be culturally- and geographically-specific, are being exchanged and shared. There is, however, a danger in assuming that healing programs working well in one context can be successfully transported to an entirely different social, cultural or political milieu. In fact, no single approach is applicable across all nations and communities. As Yava-Kamu-Harathunian notes with respect to Australia:

Conclusions

Too often the easy option is to believe, accept and then practice under the notion that what is good in treatment for some indigenous groups in Canada or elsewhere will translate as good and effective for Australian Aboriginal clients with diverse often multiple language use, from diverse cultural backgrounds, and from diverse Aboriginal lifestyles. For years programmes for Aboriginal prisoners were produced as 'by-products' of Anglo-Canadian, European, English or Anglo-American programmes. These programmes were produced in those countries for their indigenous populations. It was often assumed that in the case of the American Indian, and the First Nations peoples of Canada and New Zealand, that because of the similarities with history and involvement in the criminal justice system these treatment programmes could also be used to address the treatment needs of Aboriginal offenders (Yava-Kamu-Harathunian, 2002:21).

While adaptations and sharing of Indigenous practices take place across cultures, an increased resistance to viewing Aboriginal people as having a homogeneous set of traditions and practices is evident. At a global level, efforts are required to maintain and support the cultural diversity that currently exists. At the community level, there is some evidence that culturally-appropriate healing interventions are most effective when rooted in local practices, languages and traditions. At the same time, urbanization and the cumulative effects of assimilation policies have left many Indigenous people alienated from their land and culture and, sometimes, their family. Specific strategies are needed to meet the needs of Indigenous people who do not have strong cultural ties.

Finally, many healing programs incorporate, adapt and blend traditional and Western approaches. Traditional ceremonies, medicines and healing practices are being incorporated into the therapeutic process while Indigenous values and worldviews are providing the program framework. Some core values, such as holism, balance and connection to family and the environment, are common to Aboriginal worldviews across cultures; others are clearly rooted in local customs and traditions. The variety of therapeutic combinations in use suggests a powerful commitment to the values of adaptability, flexibility and innovation in the service of healing. This is consistent with the holistic approach to healing common to Indigenous value systems.

Holistic healing suggests that different therapies used in combination will more effectively address the healing needs of the whole person. For Indigenous people, the concept of holism extends beyond the mental, physical, emotional and spiritual aspects of individual lives to encompass relationships with families, communities and

Conclusions

the physical environment. Such approaches challenge governments that compartmentalize funding through departments (health, education, housing, etc.), but they are natural to Indigenous service providers. A holistic approach also challenges many Western medical practitioners who separate physical and mental health and do not deal with the spiritual dimension.

Culturally-sensitive screening and assessment tools that complement holistic and relational worldviews are required. These tools should include subject matter relevant to the people being assessed (e.g., Native American youth from a particular tribe or Maori living in a large urban centre). The subject matter should also include questions about spiritual connections, participation in ceremonies and connection to nature, culture, family and community.

In addition to the converging themes noted above, some lessons can be learned from the differences observed across cultures, nations and nation-states:

* The existence of treaties that are recognized and respected by government and incorporated into government policy provide an environment conducive to the development of healing programs designed, delivered and controlled by Aboriginal people. This is evident in New Zealand where the *Treaty of Waitangi* is referenced in government policy.

* Failures on the part of governments to formally recognize and affirm Indigenous rights and to accept responsibility for past policies aimed at assimilating Indigenous people is an impediment to healing, both symbolically and with respect to the development of policies and programs that support individual and community healing. This is clear from the Australian experience.

* Residential, boarding and mission schools in Canada, the United States and Australia shared a common goal of assimilating Indigenous children into the dominant culture and society. There are also some notable differences. In the United States, policy fluctuations in the 1930s and 1970s resulted in periods where more progressive attitudes prevailed toward Aboriginal culture, including ceremonial and religious practices. Also, the emphasis on extra-curricular activities in the American schools allowed team sports and Native American art, music, drama and dance to flourish.

Conclusions

• While the Canadian and Australian governments made arrangements with churches to run their institutions, most of the American schools were administered by the Bureau of Indian Affairs. A further difference is found in the accounts of former students: there are relatively fewer references to sexual abuse in American schools. While reports of sexual abuse certainly exist, the issue is not raised by former students as persistently and pervasively as in Canada or Australia. What remains unclear is whether sexual abuse was less common in schools administered by government rather than churches, or if the issue has not yet fully entered the American discourse. Further research is required to clarify this issue and to explore a possible relationship between church involvement in boarding schools and sexual abuse.

• The Western practice of documenting and evaluating therapeutic approaches and publishing the results of studies can complement traditional healing practices by providing an alternative means of knowledge transmission. This is especially effective when the researchers and authors are Indigenous people. In New Zealand, for example, an increasing number of Maori are involved in researching and writing about healing. This is not only a reflection of the growing number of Maori with professional qualifications, but also an indication that Maori knowledge about health and healing is gaining respect in its own right. The involvement of local Indigenous researchers in research and evaluation may lead to greater accountability to the community with respect to protecting traditional knowledge and following rules governing how, when and to whom this knowledge may be transmitted. Certain Western skills applied in a culturally-appropriate way are especially effective if the Western-trained professional is an Aboriginal person.

In summary, a number of similarities and differences have been noted in Indigenous approaches to healing in the United States, New Zealand, Australia and Greenland. The central lesson learned about promising healing practices is the immense value and efficacy of incorporating history and culture into holistic programs based on Indigenous values and worldviews.

References

Assembly of First Nations (AFN) (1997a). Indigenous Health Systems: A Review and Analysis of Successful Programs in Canada, US and Australia, Designed and Delivered by First Nations and Indigenous Peoples, Part I: Context and Models of Authority (DRAFT). Ottawa, ON: Assembly of First Nations.

——— (1997b). Indigenous Health Systems: A Review and Analysis of Successful Programs in Canada, US and Australia, Designed and Delivered by First Nations and Indigenous Peoples, Part II: Summary of Successful Programs (DRAFT). Ottawa, ON: Assembly of First Nations.

Archuleta, Margaret L., Brenda J. Child and K. Tsianina Lomawaima (eds.) (2000). Away from Home: American Indian Boarding School Experiences 1879-2000. Phoenix, AZ: Heard Museum.

Australia Human Rights and Equal Opportunity Commission (HREOC) (1997). Bringing Them Home: Report of the National Inquiry into the Separation of Aboriginal and Torres Strait Islander Children from Their Families. Sydney, NSW: Sterling Press Pty. Ltd. (The full report can also be retrieved from: http://www.austlii.edu.au/au/special/rsjproject/rsjlibrary/hreoc/stolen)

Australia National Health and Medical Research Council (NHMRC) (1996). Promoting the Health of Aboriginal and Torres Strait Island Communities: Case studies and principles of good practices. Canberra, AU: Australian Government Publishing Service. (This publication has been rescinded.)

Australian National Audit Office (2002). The Aboriginal and Torres Strait Islander Health Program Follow-up Audit. The Auditor-General Audit Report No. 15 Performance Audit on Department of Health and Ageing, Aboriginal and Torres Strait Islander Commission (ATSIC), 2002/2003. Tabled 29 October 2002. Retrieved from: http://www.anao.gov.au/WebSite.nsf/Publications/23817F9E309B2FB54A256C6100254991

Barnes, H.M. (2000). Kaupapa maori: explaining the ordinary. Pacific Health Dialog: Journal of Community Health and Clinical Medicine for the Pacific 7(1): 13-16.

Brown, Gwen and Marjorie Hayes (2002). Ali-Curung Presentation. Paper presented at the Reconciliation Australia Conference on The Northern Territory Aboriginal Law and Justice Strategy, April 2002. Retrieved 2 February 2004 from: http://www.reconciliationaustralia.org/docs/speeches/governance2002/12_ali_curung.doc

Bjerregaard, Peter and T. Kue Young (1998). The Circumpolar Inuit: Health of a Population in Transition. Copenhagen, DK: Munksgaard.

Bjerregaard, P., T. Curtis, K. Borch-Johnsen, G. Mulvad, U. Becker, S. Anderson and V. Backer (2003). Inuit Health in Greenland: A population survey of life style and disease in Greenland and among Inuit living in Denmark. International Journal of Circumpolar Health 62(supp. 1):1-79.

Buffalohead, W. Roger and Paulette Fairbanks Molin (2000). "A Nucleus of Civilization": families at Hampton Institute. In Archuleta, Margaret L., Brenda J. Child and K. Tsianina Lomawaima (eds.), Away from Home: American Indian Boarding School Experiences 1879-2000. Phoenix, AZ: Heard Museum: 116-133.

References

Coupe, Nicole M. (2000). Maori suicide prevention in New Zealand. Pacific Health Dialog: Journal of Community Health and Clinical Medicine for the Pacific 7(1): 25-28.

Cunningham, Chris (2000). A framework for addressing Māori knowledge in research, science and technology. Pacific Health Dialog: Journal of Community Health and Clinical Medicine for the Pacific 7(1):62-69.

Curtis, Tine, Finn B. Larsen, Karin Helweg-Larsen and Peter Bjerregaard (2002). Violence, Sexual Abuse and Health in Greenland. International Journal of Circumpolar Health 61:110-122.

Debo, Angie (1983). A History of the Indians of the United States. Norman, OK: University of Okalahoma Press (first printing in 1970).

Duran, Eduardo and Bonnie Duran (1995). Native American Postcolonial Psychology. Albany, NY: State University of New York Press.

——— (2000). Applied Postcolonial Clinical and Research Strategies. In Battiste, Marie (ed.), Reclaiming Indigenous Voice and Vision. Vancouver, BC: UBC Press: 86-100.

Durie, Mason (2000). Maori health: key determinants for the next twenty-five years. Pacific Health Dialog: Journal of Community Health and Clinical Medicine for the Pacific 7(1):6-11.

Ellison-Loschmann, Lis and Neil Pearce (2000). He Mate Huango: an update on Maori asthma. Pacific Health Dialog: Journal of Community Health and Clinical Medicine for the Pacific 7(1): 82-93.

Finkler, H. (1990). The Political Framework of Aboriginal Criminal Justice in Northern Canada. Law and Anthropology 5:113-119.

Fryer-Smith, Stephanie (2002). Aboriginal Benchbook for Western Australian courts (AIJA Model Indigenous Benchbook Project). Carleton Victoria, AU: Australian Institute of Judicial Administration Incorporated.

Gannage, Mark (1998). An International Perspective: A Review and Analysis of Approaches to Addressing Past Institutional or Systemic Abuse in Selected Countries. From CD-ROM, Law Commission of Canada (2001), Restoring Dignity: Responding to Child Abuse in Canadian Institutions.

Graham, Thomas L. Crofoot (2002). Using Reasons for Living to Connect American Indian Healing Traditions. Journal of Sociology and Social Welfare 29(1):55-75.

Green, Rayna and John Troutman (2000). "By the Waters of the Minnehaha": music and dance, pageants and princesses. In Archuleta, Margaret L., Brenda J. Child and K. Tsianina Lomawaima (eds), Away from Home: American Indian Boarding School Experiences 1879-2000. Phoenix, AZ: Heard Museum: 60-83.

Health Canada (2001). First Nations and Inuit Health System Renewal, Health Care for Indigenous People: International Experiences, Part 1 - Background (draft). Ottawa, ON: Health Canada.

References

Henderson, Ailsa (2003). Report of the Workshop on Best Practices in Suicide Prevention and the Evaluation of Suicide Prevention Programs in the Arctic, Iqaluit, Nunavut, 14-15 March, 2003. Prepared for the Government of Nunavut, Department of Executive and Intergovernmental Affairs, Evaluation and Statistics Division.

Herman, Judith (1997). Trauma and Recovery: The aftermath of violence—from domestic abuse to political terror. New York, NY: Basic Books.

Horomia, Parekura (2003). Maori Affairs Minister. Maori schools to benefit from Gateway programme. New Zealand Government press release 20/05/2003. Retrieved from: http://www.beehive.govt.nz

Huriwai, Terry, Rahul Sant Ram, Daryle Derring and J. Douglas Sellman (1998). Treatment for Maori with Alcohol and Drug Problems. In Sellman, J.D., G.M. Robinson, R. McCormick and G.M. Dore (eds.), The Long and the Short of Treatment for Alcohol and Drug Disorders. Christchurch, NZ: Department of Psychological Medicine, Christchurch School of Medicine: 32-37.

Huriwai, Terry, J. Douglas Sellman, Patrick Sullivan and Tuari L. Potiki (2000). Optimal Treatment for Maori with Alcohol and Drug-Use-Related Problems: An Investigation of Cultural Factors in Treatment. Substance Use & Misuse 35(3): 281-300.

Huriwai, Terry, Paul J. Robertson, Delaraine Armstrong, Te Pare Kingi and Paraire Huata (2001). Whanaungatanga - a process in the treatment of Maori with alcohol- and drug-use related problems. Substance Use & Misuse 36(8): 1033-1051.

Ihimaera, Witi (ed.) (1998). Growing Up Māori. Auckland, NZ: Tandem Press.

Jensen, Jette (1999). Suicide in the Arctic - Practise versus Theory. In Tedebrand, Lars-Göran and Peter Sköld (eds.) (1999), The Thirteenth Nordic Demographic Symposium, Umeå (Sweden), 15-17 August 1999. Scandinavian Population Studies, Vol. 12. Report No. 18. Retrieved 27 August 2003 from: http:www.kiip.gl/forskning/projekt/rapport/jette/tekst.htm

Jonas, William (2001). From an International Perspective: The Removal of Children and Reparations. Keynote Address, 'Healing the Pain' Stolen Generations Conference, 12-14 March 2001, Adelaide. Retrieved January 2004 from: http://www.healthinfornet.ecu.eda.au/html/html_bulletin/bull_11/stolengen.pdf.

Jones, Rhys (2000a). Diagnosis in traditional Maori healing: a contemporary urban clinic. Pacific Health Dialog: Journal of Community Health and Clinical Medicine for the Pacific 7(1):17-24.

Jones, Rhys Griffith (2000b). Rongoā Māori and Primary Health Care. A thesis submitted in partial fulfilment of the requirements for the degree of Master of Public Health, University of Auckland. Retrieved February 2004 from: http://www.hauora.com/downloads/files/Thesis-Rhys%20Griffith%20 Jones-Rongoa%20Maori%20and%20Primary%20Health%20Care.pdf

Jones, Rhys (2000c). Traditional Maori healing. Pacific Health Dialog: Journal of Community Health and Clinical Medicine for the Pacific 7(1):107-109.

References

Kishk Anaquot Health Research (2001). An Interim Evaluation Report of Aboriginal Healing Foundation Program Activity. Ottawa, ON: Aboriginal Healing Foundation.

——— (2002). Journey and Balance: Second Interim Evaluation Report of Aboriginal Healing Foundation Program Activity. Ottawa, ON: Aboriginal Healing Foundation.

——— (2003). Third Interim Evaluation Report of Aboriginal Healing Foundation Program Activity. Ottawa, ON: Aboriginal Healing Foundation.

Kotz, Dorothy (2001). Opening Speech, 12 March 2001, 'Healing the Pain' Stolen Generations Conference, 12-14 March 2001, Adelaide, AU. Retrieved January 2004 from: http://www.healthinfornet.ecu.eda.au/html/html_bulletin/bull_11/stolengen.pdf

Laenui, Poka (Hayden F. Burgess) (2000). Processes of Decolonization. In Battiste, Marie (ed.), Reclaiming Indigenous Voice and Vision. Vancouver, BC: UBC Press, 150-160.

Larsen, Jillian, Paul Robertson, David Hillman and Stephen M. Hudson (1998). Te Piriti: A Bicultural Model for Treating Child Molesters in Aotearoa/New Zealand. In Marshall, W.L., M. Stephen Hudson, Tony Ward and Y. Fernandez (eds.), Sourcebook of Treatment Programs for Sexual Offenders. New York, NY: Plenum Press: 385-398.

Leineweber, Markus and Ella Arensman (2003). Culture Change and Mental Health: The Epidemiology of Suicide in Greenland. Archives of Suicide Research 7(1):41-50.

New Zealand Ministry of Health (2002). Maori Provider Development Scheme 2002 / 2003 - Application Guidelines. Auckland, NZ: Maori Health Directorate, Ministry of Health.

——— (1999). Standards for Traditional Māori Healing. Wellington, NZ. Ministry of Health.

O'Donoghue, Lowitja (2001). I am black. I am proud. Dealing with my Identity. Keynote 9:45am, March 14th, 2001, 'Healing the Pain' Stolen Generations Conference, 12-14 March 2001, Adelaide, AU. Retrieved January 2004 from: http://www.healthinfornet.ecu.eda.au/html/html_bulletin/bull_11/stolengen.pdf

Ogunwole, Stella U. (2002). The American Indian and Alaska Native Population: 2000. Census 2000 Brief. Washington, DC: U.S. Census Bureau.

Olsen, Karl Kristian (n.d.). Education in Greenland. Alaska Native Knowledge Network. Retrieved 28 July 2003 from: http://www.ankn.uaf.edu/edgreen.html

Parker, Dorothy R. (1996). Phoenix Indian School: The Second Half-Century. Tucson, AZ: The University of Arizona Press.

Parliament of Australia (1998). House of Representatives. Standing Committee on Family and Community Affairs. Reference: Indigenous health, Adelaide. Official Hansard Report. Tuesday, 17 February 1998, Canberra, AU. Retrieved from: http://www.aph.gov.au/hansard/reps/committee/r1600.pdf

References

Petersen, Robert (1995). Colonialism as Seen from a Former Colonized Area. Arctic Anthropology 32(2):118-126. Retrieved 28 August 2003 from: http://arcticcircle.uconn.edu/HistoryCulture/petersen.html

Pipi, Kataraina, Fiona Cram, Rene Hawke, Sharon Hawke, Te Miringa Huriwai, Tania Mataki, Moe Milne, Karen Morgan, Huhana Tuhaka and Colleen Tuuta (2002). A Research Ethic for Studying Māori and Iwi Provider Success. Auckland, NZ. IRI: The University of Auckland. Retrieved from: http://www.arts.auckland.ac.nz/iri/mps per cent20folder.index.html

Reconciliation Australia (2002). Words, Symbols and Actions: Reconciliation Report Card 2002. A report from Reconciliation Australia to the Australian people. Retrieved from: http://www.reconciliationaustralia.org/upload/words_symbols_actions.pdf

Reid, Papaarangi, Bridget Robson and Camara Phyllis Jones (2000). Disparities in health: common myths and uncommon truths. Pacific Health Dialog: Journal of Community Health and Clinical Medicine for the Pacific 7(1):38-47.

Robertson, Paul, Jillian Larsen, David Hillman and Stephen Hudson (1999). Conceptual Issues in Therapy with Sexually Abusive Maori Men. In Lewis, Alvin D. (ed.), Cultural Diversity in Sexual Abuser Treatment: Issues and Approaches. Burlington, VT: Safer Society Press, 188-214.

Royal Commission on Aboriginal Peoples (RCAP) (1996). Report of the Royal Commission on Aboriginal Peoples, Volume 3, Gathering Strength. Ottawa, ON: Minister of Supply and Services Canada.

Skye, Warren (2002). E.L.D.E.R.S Gathering for Native American Youth: Continuing Native Traditions and Curbing Substance Abuse in Native American Youth. Journal of Sociology and Social Welfare 29(1):117-135.

Smith, Linda Tuhiwai (1999). Kaupapa Maori Methodology: Our Power to define ourselves. A seminar presentation to the School of Education, University of British Columbia. Retrieved from: http://www.hauora.com/downloads/files/ACF30AC.pdf

Statistics New Zealand (1998). New Zealand Now: Māori. Wellington, NZ: Statistics New Zealand.

Szasz, Margaret Connell (1999). Education and the American Indian: The Road to Self-Determination Since 1928, 3rd edition. Albuquerque, NM: University of New Mexico Press.

Tauri, Juan Marcellus (1998). Family Group Conferencing: The Myth of Indigenous Empowerment in New Zealand. Justice as Healing Newsletter 4(1). Retrieved 14 March 2003 from: http://www.usask.ca/nativelaw/publications/jah/tauri.html

United States Department of Health and Human Services (1999). Surgeon General's Report, Fact Sheet: Native American Indians. Retrieved March 2004 from: http://www.mentalhealth.org/cre/fact4.asp

Wesley-Esquimaux, Cynthia C. and Magdalena Smolewski (2004). Historic Trauma and Aboriginal Healing. Ottawa, ON: Aboriginal Healing Foundation.

References

Whitmore, Robbie (n.d.). New Zealand in History: The Māori. Retrieved from: http://history-nz-org/maori7.html

Woods, Teri Knutson, Karen Blaine and Lauri Francisco (2002). O'odham Himdag as a Source of Strength and Wellness Among the Tohono O'odham of Southern Arizona and Northern Sonora, Mexico. Journal of Sociology and Social Welfare 29(1):35-53.

Yavu-Kama-Harathunian, Cheri (2002). The Therapeutic Needs of Indigenous Violent and Sex Offending Males: How Can They Be Addressed. Treatment issues related to criminogenic factors of aboriginal group participants outside the domain of group programme delivery. Paper presented at the Probation and Community Corrections: Making the Community Safer Conference, Perth, 23-24 September 2002. Crime Research Centre, University of Western Australia. Retrieved January 2004 from: http://www.aic.gov.au/conferences/probation/yavu.pdf

Yazzie, Robert (2000). Indigenous People and Postcolonial Colonialism. In Battiste, Marie (ed.), Reclaiming Indigenous Voice and Vision. Vancouver, BC: UBC Press, 39-49.